AUTHORITY IN TRANSFORMATION

A Convoco Edition

CORINNE MICHAELA FLICK (ED.)

Convoco! Editions

Convoco Foundation
Brienner Strasse 28
D – 80333 Munich
www.convoco.co.uk

British Library Cataloguing-in-Publication data: a catalogue
record for this book is available from the British Library.

Edited by Dr. Corinne Michaela Flick
Translated from German by Philippa Hurd
Layout and typesetting by Jill Sawyer Phypers
Printed and bound in Great Britain by Clays Ltd., St Ives plc

ISBN: 978-0-9931953-4-1

Previously published Convoco titles:

Power and its Paradoxes (2016)

To Do or Not To Do—Inaction as a Form of Action (2015)

Dealing with Downturns: Strategies in Uncertain Times (2014)

Collective Law-Breaking—A Threat to Liberty (2013)

Who Owns the World's Knowledge? (2012)

**Can't Pay, Won't Pay? Sovereign Debt and the Challenge of
Growth in Europe (2011)**

Authority. *Man cannot exist without it, an• yet it brings in its train just as much of error as of truth.*

—*Johann Wolfgang von Goethe (1749–1832)*

CONTENTS

INTRODUCTION

Dear Friends of Convoco,

When it comes to finding Convoco's annual topic, I always try to think ahead: what is likely to become so socially relevant in the coming year that it merits discussion in a substantial and interdisciplinary way? Fortunately, serendipity has usually guided the choice.

Rarely has a topic proved to be more relevant, as it evolved over the course of the year, than "Authority in Question." All over the world, traditional structures of authority are in a state of upheaval. The establishment, once regarded as a guarantor of constancy, has been punished and voted out of office. New sources of authority are emerging, and we do not yet know how they will evolve. This book shines a light on this change and investigates it thoroughly.

The structure of Convoco has also experienced a change of authority in the form of expansion. Alongside authoritative figures from the traditional disciplines of science, politics, law, and economics, which are often represented in this book, the Convoco Forum has welcomed for the first time new authorities from the digital world—startup entrepreneurs and academics such as Bruce Pon, Julie Maupin, Garrick Hileman, and Marcella Atzori. A change in patterns of authority is taking place as a result of the growing digitization of our society. It is essential that we consciously face up to this change and integrate it, otherwise the fact that governing authorities are ignoring doubts about globalization, for example, may lead to the kind of loss of authority we are currently witnessing.

When societies become increasingly alienated from their governments and dissatisfaction grows, people look for alternatives. The use of achievements in the digital field such as blockchain technology is such an alternative. Its consequences can be negative as well as positive. This new technology can undermine the authority of the banks or circumvent the usual monitoring of currency exchanges carried out by states—with results that may be good or ill, according to circumstances. On the positive side, intellectual property can be protected in ways that are independent of state regulation. People who are trapped behind borders, who cannot vote, or who have no passport, can at last become financially independent of their states' currency systems through blockchain technologies such as Bitcoin.

At the same time, decentralization through technology poses risks. Often, new technologies such as blockchain, for example, are praised for their transparency and democratic nature, but these do not exist in a neutral space, independent of an existing power structure. Once again, it is the case that the more knowledge, the more know-how there is, the more there is power to be derived from the control over such technological developments. Thus, it is possible that, under cover of transparency, a technocratic system may be created that is neither more democratic nor more transparent than the existing structures—and which may be substantially worse.

For centuries, within the international social order, we have developed laws to regulate our coexistence. Bitcoin began as a lawless space that consciously wanted to distance itself from governments and authority. However, the blockchain technology on which Bitcoin depends, like so many other achievements of the digital world, cannot and should not operate in isolation from existing legal structures. A link between the digital world and the real world must be created. This link should be created by the law.

As Peter M. Huber, Christoph Paulus, Wolfgang Schön, and Peter Maurer each points out in their contributions, however, the law itself does not escape conflicts of authority. Increasingly, its validity is being undermined and called into question. In his essay, "The Authority of the Law in Flux," Peter M. Huber makes it clear that instances where actors in the political sphere have disregarded the law or have failed to accept some measure of containment by the law have seriously increased over recent years. In this way, citizens' confidence in the integrity of institutions may be damaged in the long term. The state under the rule of law [*Rechtsstaat*] exists through the law or it does not exist at all.[1] As Christoph Paulus observes in his essay "Does the Law Still have Authority?" the rule of law is the greatest guarantee of individual freedom. This foundation must be preserved. This means an ongoing engagement with the legal foundations of our societies and careful attention to ensuring that what is built upon them is fit for purpose in our contemporary world. In his contribution, Wolfgang Schön argues that the challenges posed to the functioning of the rule of law have increased steadily over the last few decades (for example, through new legal sectors developing in the realms of cyberspace and digitization). This growing complexity, he suggests, needs to be managed through a better understanding of the law itself. Citizens must be given clarity. There can be no rule of law without the capacity required to comprehend and apply the rule of law.

In order to preserve stability and a functioning society, governmental authority must deal with emerging sources of potentially rival authority in all their guises, and try to meet challenges through better explanation and guidance. This is how new actors and new areas of knowledge that constitute competing sources of authority can be integrated into our present systems. We need to be able to manage change so that authority can take on new forms, without faith either in the democratic system of government or in the workings of the rule of law breaking down.

Corinne Michaela Flick, January 2017

Note

1   Peter M. Huber in "The Authority of the Law in Flux."

THESES

_____

CORINNE M. FLICK

Those who have authority have responsibility—the more authority, the greater the responsibility.

ROGER SCRUTON

The conferring of authority may be by election or by the assumption of an historical office according to the requirements of law. But there is no office without the responsibilities that define it, and to exercise power outside the limits set by those responsibilities is to act, as the law puts it, *ultra vires*—beyond the powers conferred. This view of government tells us that politics is not about power but about authority, and that authority comes when people are accountable, directly or indirectly, to others who have less power than themselves.

CLEMENS FUEST

Today authority means less than ever that politicians merely decide and the citizens follow. In spite of this, the hope that referenda would lead to politics being more strongly focused on the interests of citizens quickly turns to illusion, when referenda are abused by governments for strategic purposes, as happens again and again at the moment. Plebiscites should have a clearly defined place in the constitutional system, and initiatives for referenda should come, first and foremost, from the people, not from governments.

STEFAN KORIOTH

Democracy needs authority and it must radiate authority, but it is not allowed to be authoritarian. Its greatest threat today lies in its development into a "game without citizens," in which there is no one to give democracy authority, and where citizens do not have a sense of authority.

WOLFGANG SCHÖN

The law lives through its authority. This authority is not restricted to the law being obeyed by the citizen.

Before it can be respected and obeyed by the citizen, the law must also be understood, explained, and its meaning recognized in each individual case. To do this both state and society must possess capacities—personal, financial, and intellectual—otherwise there is a danger of the law causing crippling anxiety or a risky escape into the unknown.

CHRISTOPH G. PAULUS

While the law should be understood as an imperative and a principle for all future cases, politics adapts to the needs and requirements of the day. This antagonism between law and politics is undermined when laws are formulated in such a way that an action operating against the proclaimed intention is possible; for in this way the law orients itself according to the requirements of politics and, with it, is in danger of losing its authority. At the same time it is thereby deprived of one of its most valuable characteristics, namely its ability to anticipate certain outcomes.

PETER M. HUBER

Unconditional respect for the authority of the law is part of Germany's national identity. It has grown up over centuries and has led to a wide variety of "entries in our collective dictionary." The authority of the law has suffered. Under the conditions of globalization, European integration, and the overlapping of state powers, the core of the state under the rule of law, namely the containment of politics by law (Kant), has become ineffective.

PETER MAURER

Rebuilding consensus on the validity and importance of the law and the principles of humanitarian action will be crucial. This is why ICRC considers its frontline engagement and negotiations with parties to conflicts with the objective of respecting the norms and opening humanitarian spaces the most important humanitarian contribution to rebuilding authority in society.

THOMAS HOEREN

The digital transformation is in full swing. The changes affect not only the areas of "digital" law such as information law, IT law, data protection, or telecommunications law, but the law as a whole. For example, in the case of the German Civil Code [BGB] traditional civil law too is being put to the test. In the background there lurks the question of what demands big data will make of constitutional law.

STEFAN OSCHMANN

Is authority losing its relevance? Although it seems paradoxical, the contrary is the case. Changing social values, volatile economies and financial markets, and fast-paced technological progress can pose serious challenges to established organizations in all sectors. Dealing with these factors requires effective leadership. It requires authority, but in a more inclusive sense.

KAI A. KONRAD

In the short term, there are many factors that determine a country's economic development. One of these factors is psychology. Economic development frequently requires similar or complementary actions to be taken by many economic actors. Consequently, trust in the actions of others, and with it trust in economic recovery or the stability of the economic climate, play a decisive role. In this situation the authority of the press comes into the frame.

CLAUDIA M. BUCH

In the past we have repeatedly seen phases of liberalization and phases during which the opening up of markets was once again rolled back. In response to the serious financial crisis which began in 2007/08 we have reacted by strengthening international cooperation, developing new institutions, and better regulation of the financial markets. This means that we are better equipped today than in the past to deal with current market challenges.

RICHARD WENTWORTH

I love a good detective and my own ability to make a judgment is at the center of my self-esteem. I look out for original minds and people who convey their own experience with flair. Somewhere in this mixture lies my sense of authority. I enormously appreciate those who "know" more than me.

CHAPTER 1

THOUGHTS ON AUTHORITY

CORINNE M. FLICK AND CLEMENS FUEST

What role does authority play in society today? Authority as a mere exercise of power over others without their consent should no longer have a place in free, democratic societies. But authority is much more. Through merit, personal effectiveness, and other qualities, people can become authorities who provide guidance and command trust. A politician such as Helmut Schmidt had personal authority, as he proved his leadership qualities in crises such as the North Sea flood of 1962 or during the height of Red Army Faction terrorism in fall 1977. An institution such as Germany's Bundesbank has authority because it has proven its worth as a guarantor of a stable currency over many decades. Likewise, Germany's Federal Constitutional Court has authority, not primarily because it can rein in parliaments and governments, but because citizens trust the Court to defend them against infringements of their basic rights, even against the capriciousness of state authorities. Authority, understood in this way, is based on consent and acceptance by all concerned. It is always, therefore, conditional.

Max Weber linked the question of authority to that of legitimacy. Our state authority is characterized by the fact that it is legitimized by consent. If power is based on force, it loses its claim on legitimate authority. A population accepts governmental authority if it has been acquired through elections. Like other countries in the West, Germany is a representative democracy. Through elections, the citizens transfer responsibility and authority to their representatives.

This voluntarily granted form of authority can, of course, change over time—it is fragile and mutable. While it has a formal basis—for example, in the election of a member of parliament—it also needs to be complemented by acceptance by the electors and the general public. It usually takes a long time for an institution or person to gain real authority, but it can be quickly lost. Politicians or economic policy-makers who break laws or have to answer for blatant failures can lose all authority in a matter of days or even hours.

The sudden loss of people's authority can be traumatic for those affected. For society as a whole, however, the damage is usually limited, and not only because office-holders can be replaced. Indeed, it is actually desirable that the power linked to authority persists only so long as it is legitimized by the consent of others. In recent political decision-making processes—such as the Brexit referendum or the nomination of Donald Trump as a candidate for the US presidency and his ultimate election victory—many people see a disturbing deterioration of the authority of established political institutions. On the positive side, however, we can also take the view that the established parties have strayed too far from the wishes of the people. If they change their behavior, they have the opportunity of winning back their authority.

This volume has been deliberately titled *Authority in Transformation*, rather than *Authority in Crisis*. We do not see that the authority of our democratic system has been completely undermined. Churchill's famous quotation that "the best argument against democracy is a five-minute conversation with the average voter" hints at the limitations involved in letting complex and substantive issues be decided by plebiscites, but it does not place democracy itself in doubt. However, we must confront the fact that we are being faced with a change in the way authority functions within the state and this has consequences for our understanding of democracy. The old order is being subjected to evolutionary, if not yet revolutionary, change.

As an example, let us take representative democracy in its current form. It retains very little in common with the original democracy of Ancient Greece, which was characterized by action without mediation, without representation. However, it is also no longer the democracy of 1949 when Germany's Basic Law [*Grun⸱gesetz*] came into being. Today the citizens want to take part in the political process.

In an age of instant communication and real-time opinion polls, purely representative democracy seems no longer to satisfy today's demands and needs, as the impression has arisen that the representative system and the major parties have not taken the requirement for participation seriously. This has engendered a feeling of powerlessness among many citizens that has led to a desire for more direct democracy.

When we talk about authority, the impression can easily arise that more authority means less freedom. Authority is often equated with what Kant famously called heteronomy—the individual's subjection to an external force or will, and the opposite of autonomy. However, if authority is based on a broad consensus, there exists a benign relationship of cooperation between authority and freedom. Freedom can only be enjoyed under certain general conditions. It is the task of authority to set these conditions so that freedom can be maintained. A loss of authority does not automatically correspond to a gain in freedom. Authority does not necessarily act in opposition to freedom.

Perhaps the most striking development of the last decade is that we can see a trend towards the dissolution, or challenging, of hierarchies in favor of ever-higher levels of participation. More people would like to be actively involved in political decision-making processes. Many of the demands moving in this direction recall Jean-Jacques Rousseau's idea of a radical democracy. A fundamental change in our understanding of democracy is taking place. We are moving towards a multi-level democracy, towards a "multiple democracy," as historian Paul Nolte calls it. One example is the courts of law. More and more frequently citizens are applying directly to the courts, rather than taking the indirect route via institutions and parliaments. At EU level, too, we can observe this form of "judicial democracy."[1] In this context we can cite the action brought against the European Central

Bank's decision on Outright Monetary Transactions:[2] for the first time in constitutional history, voters—not organs of the state—opposed the measures of an EU institution.

However, we also observe that institutions are losing their authority. Such a loss is, in part, more serious for society at large than the loss of authority is for political figures. Institutions are undergoing change, but in spite of this they should remain stable, long-term organizations. By contrast with politicians— who can be voted in and out, who gain authority and can then lose it again—institutions such as courts, central banks, and competition authorities form the foundations of state systems and the framework for international cooperation (the EU and NATO are cases in point). In times when the call for citizens to have direct influence is becoming ever louder, institutions are suffering from the democratic deficit of which they are often accused. Of course in their remit they are politically neutral, but this also means that they exist outside direct democratic control and can easily appear remote from the people.

On the other hand, new types of institutions, offering public participation in extra-parliamentary representative bodies and non-state institutions, such as Greenpeace and Attac, are emerging.[3] The call for more direct democracy and a transformation of our understanding of authority stands for a new kind of quest for stability and authority, wherein at the same time citizens aspire to autonomous, direct responsibility.

At first glance, plebiscites and referenda are processes in which citizens can be involved in political decisions most directly. There are democracies (such as Switzerland) in which plebiscites have a long tradition, and are regarded not as the antithesis of representative democracy, but as its complement.

In the last resort, however, we must consider which questions are suitable to be decided directly by the citizens. For example: was the question posed in the Brexit referendum a decision that could sensibly be made by the general public directly, and could that general public in any way do justice to the responsibility that went with the choice? In the case of various referenda in recent years, we must question whether they have really improved citizens' participation in the political decision-making process. To a large extent, the Brexit referendum was an instrument for the Prime Minister, David Cameron, to maintain his power in the Conservative Party, first and foremost, and then to pressurize the other members of the EU into meeting British demands.

In Greece, Prime Minister Alexis Tsipras used the referendum on the restructuring program as an instrument for implementing his demands for concessions from his nation's creditors.

Plebiscites also easily turn into polls about issues that are not being voted on at all—as in Italy on December 4, 2016, when the people were supposed to be deciding about constitutional reform, but it seems that in reality they were passing judgement on the then Prime Minister, Matteo Renzi, and his policies.

Today, attitudes towards authority mean that, less than ever, can politicians assume that they merely decide and the citizens will follow. Yet, in spite of this, the hope that referenda would lead to politics being more strongly focused on the interests of citizens has quickly turned out to be an illusion; referenda are abused by governments for different political purposes, as has happened in the past and is happening again and again at the moment. Plebiscites should have a clearly defined place in the constitutional system, and initiatives for referenda should come, first and foremost, from the people, not from governments. This requires defined conditions for their use and exacting thresholds for the successful adoption of a proposal.

Notes

1. Cf. Paul Nolte, *Was ist Demokratie? Geschichte und Gegenwart* (Munich: C.H. Beck, 2012), p. 388.

2. Outright Monetary Transactions are instruments for purchasing short-term bonds from states in the Eurozone.

3. Paul Nolte, "Postdemokratie? Von der repräsentativen zur multiplen Demokratie" in *Aus Politik und Zeitgeschichte*, 1–2/2011, p. 10.

CHAPTER 2

AUTHORITY FOR TODAY'S BUSINESS WORLD

STEFAN OSCHMANN

For centuries, the concept of authority in business was well-defined. It meant surveilling subordinates, enforcing one's own decisions and exercising power. Those at the top of an organization were the undisputed masters of their company. Orders had to be adhered to, and not questioned. However, over the last couple of years, we have increasingly seen businesses missing out on fundamental trends, damaging their reputation, losing market share, or even going bankrupt because of fatal decisions by management that were carried out unquestioned. In these cases, at least to a certain extent, authority was part of the problem. Given these developments, everyone who holds or aspires to hold a management position in any kind of organization should reflect on the concept of authority.

The concept of authority has always played a central role in the social sciences and humanities. There is an abundance of literature and definitions. From the time of Plato and Aristotle until today, philosophers have been debating the legitimate extent of political rule. The term authority itself can be traced back to Ancient Rome. Romans spoke of *auctoritas* to describe a certain level of prestige a person had achieved and, as a consequence, his ability to rally support around his will. In modern times, the German sociologist Max Weber developed the concept of authority further by offering an influential classification into rational-legal, traditional, and charismatic types. The works of the Frankfurt School then paved the way for the fundamental criticism of authority by the members of the counterculture generation of the 1960s.

Today, social scientists seek new concepts. Haim Omer, psychologist at Tel Aviv University proposes a "new authority" which centers on the idea of "vigilant care." It therefore seems safe to conclude that authority will certainly remain a subject of debate among academics.

But with regard to modern business organizations, one fundamental question arises: do we need authority at all? At a first glance the companies that appear to be most successful in today's economy are those that actively dismiss it; for example, biotech start-ups which focus their limited resources on research and nothing else, or Google in its early days. The company started out without rules and without a plan. Early on, this had enormous benefits. The company was extremely innovative and flexible.

But while authority can be forgone in order to spur innovation, it is vital when it comes to managing a business. The former start-up Google is today a company with more than 60,000 employees and sales of almost US$ 75 billion.[1] So it is clear that it simply can't function anymore without rules. Once a certain size is reached, *every* enterprise requires hierarchies, structures, and rules. Every enterprise requires authority.

If nobody sets objectives and values, then there will be nobody who is prepared to take responsibility afterwards. Almost everyone who has worked in a large organization, in business, government, or the non-profit sector has probably experienced this principle of organized irresponsibility at some point in time. It is likely to occur when organizations have reached or exceeded a certain size and a certain degree of complexity. For example, nowadays large corporations often operate in a global matrix structure across national borders. This has clear benefits. It facilitates communication and it allows complex challenges to be tackled. But when not managed properly, matrix structures can lead to difficulties with authority and responsibility. Employees no longer know exactly who is actually responsible for what. As a consequence, downright disorientation and often self-resignation as well take hold.

All too often, this results in the uncertain and bad feeling among employees that one's own work has no impact. An organization in that kind of situation can be compared to a large ship drifting on the high seas without a navigator or captain; it's not sinking, but it doesn't have a clear course either. Companies that engage in competitive markets cannot afford to become trapped in such a situation of organized irresponsibility—at least not over a long period of time.

On the contrary: competitive markets demand a workforce that is dedicated and driven to achieving the projected business goals.

This is not possible without authority. The question is merely what actually is authority? How does it work? And how can the concept of authority be adapted to a world that is changing fundamentally?

Taking stock, it quickly becomes evident that there are completely different kinds of authority. There is the institutional authority, for example, that used to be taught in the army. Modern armies do not apply this concept anymore. But for centuries they followed one simple principle: "Rank is everything"—here it was simply about how many stars or stripes you had on your uniform. With this kind of authority, content played no part. The supervisor could give whatever order he liked—it had to be adhered to, simply because he was the supervisor.

Institutional authority certainly still plays an important role in all large organizations with steep hierarchies. Its persistence is backed by the fact that many people at least sometimes are prone to overestimate authority. In fact, this willingness to recognize authority is probably more the rule than the exception. The findings of brain research in this area are clear: people accept and follow authority—simply because it creates order, because it saves time and makes things easier.

Authority is an effective way of reducing complexity. It is therefore not only favored in organizational contexts, but is in fact unavoidable. It even emerges where management is expressly determined to avoid authority. A group of people only needs a few seconds to make someone from their ranks an "authority." Studies have shown this time and again.

This also proves an important basic principle when it comes to the maxim: "you don't have authority; it is granted to you," which holds true even with respect to the authority of the Chief Executive Officer—the position in the organization chart alone does not grant authority.

Even as CEO, for someone to truly become an authority, others must be willing to follow him or her. Shareholders, employees, and customers must be convinced that the person at the top helps them to attain their individual goals.

Authority, at least the kind that does not rest on coercion, depends on trust. People are especially willing to grant authority to others when they believe that these people have shown they are "worthy" of the trust being placed in them. In fact, in the past it has become clear time and again just how quickly such trust can be lost. And we have seen that once the trust is gone, authority also slips away—today more than ever before.

In June 2016, the British people defied all authorities by predominantly voting in favor of exiting from the European Union, despite the appeal by many government representatives and the main opposition parties to vote "remain"; despite the predictions of major economic institutions, such as the International Monetary Fund, that leaving the EU would have serious consequences for Britain's economy; and despite all facts and data which clearly stated that the United Kingdom had benefited greatly from EU membership.

The vote in favor of Brexit points to a very substantial development that affects all realms of political, economic, and social life—and that requires a new concept of authority. This development is what the former editor-in-chief of *Foreign Policy* magazine, Moises Naim, calls the decay of power. Power, Naim argues, has been fundamentally altered.

What makes him come to this conclusion? More and more people across the world are educated and healthy. They are mobile and make use of digital technology. And their values have changed; they take nothing for granted anymore. So according to Naim, power nowadays is easier to get, harder to use, and easier to lose.

Powerful institutions such as states or big corporations are increasingly put under pressure by relatively small, agile organizations and social movements. In business, large multinational companies face the mounting risk of losing their market positions to agile and aggressive start-ups, as in the case of Kodak. The company was a leading provider of cameras and photography equipment for decades. Yet, despite all its market power, Kodak underestimated the impact of digital photography and the rise of smartphones—even though it actually invented digital photography. Consequently, the company had to file for bankruptcy in 2012. That was the same year that Facebook decided to pay US$1 billion for a small start-up that had developed an app to take, edit, and share pictures with smartphones. That start-up was Instagram.

Today, practically every established enterprise faces the threat of sharing Kodak's fate. Companies in almost every industry are confronted with new players who seek to disrupt conventional value chains and define entirely new business models. That trend is very obvious in banking and finance and in the automotive industry, and it also applies to the pharmaceutical and chemical industries.

The likelihood that a company will fall from its standing at the top of its league has increased. According to a recent study, the lifespan of a corporation listed in the S&P 500 index has dropped from 67 years in the 1920s to 15 years today.[2] Another study predicts that in the next ten years, 40 percent of Fortune 500 companies will be gone.[3]

These few examples all illustrate that institutional authority is being challenged. The barriers to obtaining it, which once shielded those in privileged positions, have been significantly lowered. The spot at the top has become more slippery. Consequently, new opportunities arise for small players, at the expense of stability. Gridlock or even chaos are looming as threats in a world with less clear power structures.

Everyone who holds a position of influence and responsibility, be it in politics, in business, or in science, must accept the fact that what has long been taken for granted is increasingly being questioned. And there is no way back to the good old days of undisputed institutional authority. Hence, elites must demonstrate a certain humbleness towards the changing nature of power and—with it—of authority.

So is authority losing its relevance? Although it seems paradoxical, the contrary is the case. Changing social values, volatile economies and financial markets, and fast-paced technological progress can pose serious challenges to established organizations in all sectors. Dealing with these factors requires effective leadership. It requires authority, but in a more inclusive sense.

Authority in today's world must be less about establishing order by setting boundaries. Rather, it is about providing orientation by integrating people into the bigger picture. It is about conveying a sense of meaning. That applies to all organizations, from global philanthropies such as the Gates Foundation to corporations such as Merck. Our employees of course work for money, like everyone else. But what really drives them is a passion for science and technology: the prospect of making a difference in the fight against diseases such as cancer, of developing new tools for gene editing, and of creating even more efficient display technologies.

In order to effectively convey their specific sense of meaning, organizations or managers must exhibit a high degree of reflection and an abundance of empathy, of sensitivity for the individual.

This is why it is so important for managers to strive to be good communicators and to consider the emotional side of the people they are talking to, regardless of whether they are within or outside the boundaries of their particular organization.

Within the company, executives need to ask themselves the following question: how do we view employees? As people merely carrying out orders, as the objects of objectives and planned projects? Or as independent beings who evolve within the framework of the company and who are able to contribute their own ideas for the benefit of the entire enterprise? In the dialogue with external stakeholders, managers must decide which stance they want to take: that of an organization with no interest in broader issues without immediate relevance to its business; or that of an engaged partner eager to make a difference?

Indeed, Frank Baumann-Habersack, a management consultant, speaks in this context of a paradigm shift that is changing management relationships. He says, "A management relationship can also be one on equal terms, without giving up leadership. This idea decouples authority from subordination; it allows for equality."[4]

However, he also says, "Authority is important— specifically, authority in the sense of relationship structures that organize, integrate, are present, set boundaries, and provide protection."[5]

This concept of authority meets the requirements of today's markets. But it is much more difficult to gain and maintain this "new" form of authority, which is required to lead a company. It does not come from simply being appointed to an office or from receiving an impressive title. It cannot be obtained by making a few superficial improvements and otherwise ignoring the rules for building trust.

Instead, this "new authority" has to be earned every day through constructive interaction with others. This is demanding as it requires managers to reconcile two leadership styles: collaborative and authoritarian. This is a paradox that executives must deal with. Yet it is crucial, since meaning can best be created and communicated as a group—and perhaps only as a group.

The major advantage, however, is that managers no longer have to prove their authority and can instead shape it in cooperation with others. And they can focus on their real challenge: staying ahead of the competition in a business world that knows fewer and fewer barriers to power.

This article is based on a speech given by Stefan Oschmann on July 29, 2016, as part of the Convoco Forum in Salzburg.

Notes

1. Data referring to FY 2015 business results.
2. http://www.theatlantic.com/business/archive/2015/04/where-do-firms-go-when-they-die/390249/ (accessed July 1, 2016).

3. http://www.deloittedigital.com/us/blog/find-your-disruptive-advantage (accessed July 1, 2016).

4. http://www.changex.de/Article/interview_baumann_autoritaet_neu_denken (accessed July 1, 2016).

5. Ibid.

CHAPTER 3

AUTHORITY IN DEMOCRACY

STEFAN KORIOTH

I.

Does such a thing as authority exist in a democracy? Whoever denies this, for example by making the point that democracy is characterized precisely by the principle of self-determination and the refusal of authoritarian forms of government, as well as being based on decision-making by all, falls short of the mark. Of course authority exists in a democracy—authority understood as a particular characteristic and ability of a person or group, but also as a task for institutions.

What is more, if democracy is a form of government that relies on being constantly tested in day-to-day problem-solving, and on approval and trust, then it is clear that the definition and assignment of authority should be given a prominent position. Authority is an important source of trust and acceptance. We shall try to show this in this essay, by first defining the essence of the democratic form of government and the role of authority in it. Then our focus will move almost by default to the dependence of democratic procedures and convictions upon a particular moment in time, and the contemporary problem areas of democracy.

II.

All democracies worthy of the name pay homage to a fundamental theorem which was coined in the 18th century and which can indeed be found verbatim in many democratic constitutions ever since: all state authority is derived from the people. Despite its formulation in the indicative, this principle of the sovereignty of the people is an imperative. Every law, every act of government, every court ruling must be attributable to the people as the starting point of state authority. In this context, the German Federal Constitutional Court uses the image of a chain of legitimation:

"In a free democracy all state authority is derived from the people. It is exercised by the people in elections and votes and through specific legislative, executive, and judicial bodies. [...] To do this all organs and agencies that exercise state authority require legitimation that is derived from all the citizens as the state population [...]. This constitutionally required democratic legitimation demands an uninterrupted chain of legitimation from the people to those organs and office-holders who have been entrusted with the tasks of state."[1]

To make this possible, the democratic form of government demands rules of procedure that must satisfy three requirements.[2] It requires a rule-based and formalized decision-making procedure in which all citizens participate freely and equally and to which in principle all objects pertaining to state and society are subject and can be decided on a majority basis. In this way a continuous process of input, procedure, and output arises, which is shaped by rules and institutions without being identical with the latter. An element of democratic ethos through a focus on the common good must be added:

"Only when the majority is the result of a free, open, regularly updated opinion-forming and will-forming process in which all citizens of voting age can in principle enjoy equal rights, when they bear in mind the continually determining common good in making their decisions, in particular taking into account the rights and interests of the minority as well, and in addition not removing or restricting their legal opportunities of becoming tomorrow's majority, only then can the decision of the majority be considered the will of all in the exercise of state authority, becoming an obligation on all people according to the idea of free self-determination of all citizens."[3]

The strength of democracy lies in a reliance on participation and acceptance. At the same time that is its weakness. A democracy can make provision for mechanisms of control and protection. It cannot guarantee its own existence. If participation, acceptance, and trust are lacking, for whatever reasons, concrete democracy is the loser. Ernest Renan called the nation a "plébiscite de tous les jours."[4] This is true of democracy as well.

What is authority? Sociologically speaking it is the constitution of a relationship between people. Authority is the ability to influence or determine the behavior of another person, because the other accepts or must accept it. In the history of ideas our contemporary understanding of authority derives from two sources. The first can be traced back to Ancient Rome. *Auctoritas* is experience, superiority, and the resulting indirect power to advise. It lends weight and persuasiveness to the action of another person without being mandatory action itself. *Auctoritas* is moral pre-eminence, *potestas* is political power; in the Roman Republic *auctoritas* belongs to the Senate, while *potestas* belongs to the consuls and praetors. In modern European history what was separate in Ancient Rome comes together. When Thomas Hobbes says that "auctoritas, non veritas facit legem" he means that it is not substantive reason but the ruler's potential to power that turns a will into a generally binding law whose observance can be compelled using physical force if necessary. The rise of secular law, of law that has been emancipated from theological roots and divine commandments, leads to the combination of law, power, and authority. Since the American and French Revolutions at the end of the 18th century the law has had authority, and power is authority. In 19th-century Germany, which provided the monarchical principle with increasingly democratic elements and took a positivistic direction in legal ideas, this led to the equation of domination [*Herrschaft*] with authority.[5] Whatever is not will, cannot be expressed by law and policy. One obvious consequence can be seen in the Weimar Republic. A democracy where debate took place, where decisions were made without hierarchy or streamlined organization, which even gave a voice to its declared enemies, seemed to relativize all certainties, appearing weak and as the "negation of authority."[6] We have broken free from this in favor of another understanding of authority.

I suggest that today we should characterize the relationship between authority and democracy thus: it is not a question of where state authority comes from—this question has been answered: state authority is derived from the people. It is also not a question of repressing domination—domination exists in democracy as in other forms of government. It is also not a question of the quality of the content and the well-founded and rational form of decisions—even democracy permits irrational elements; a political conviction should be substantiated but does not have to be, and the right of all to participation and the principle of the majority preclude the domination of experts. In a democracy authority means the consistent ability to identify, process, and make decisions about problems while taking account of the above three main elements: free and equal participation of all, regulated process, and reference to potentially all the issues that affect the life of the community. Authority combines the engagement of the citizen, rational processes including supervisory bodies, problem-solving capacities of the political apparatus, and acceptance of the decision that has been made. Authority is associated with power, but it is more than power. For example, by law Germany's Federal Chancellor is given a prominent position within the German cabinet by virtue of his or her authority to issue guidelines. Whether this authority can be used depends on political configurations and the incumbent's individual powers of persuasion. The Federal President has no power; he is dependent on the authority of his person and his word. Democracy must be underpinned with authority; but a managed democracy is not a democracy.

III.

Constitutional democracy is not a timeless model of social organization but is associated with a certain period. It arose in theory from the late 17th century onwards. It was first put into practice—with lots of limitations from our contemporary point of view— in the US and France at the end of the 18th century. In spite of many setbacks, dictatorships, and pseudo-democracies, the 20th century was the century that saw the global triumph of democratic forms of government—except that what has come into being can disappear again. The democratic form of the state is not the end of history. The everyday plebiscite of democracy can break down; the democratic form of the state can fall into permanent disrepute. Today the time-based nature of democracy is also referred to by those who maintain we already live in a "post-democratic age,"[7] characterized by the "disempowerment" of the democratic process and democratically legitimized governments through the anonymous and apocryphal powers of the market, transnational companies, and supranational institutions. This focuses our attention on the current challenges that can be described equally as problems of authority.

1. A first problem area that leads to a loss of authority and leadership resides in the fact that democracies today (can) no longer decide all of society's questions. Supranationally, transnationally, and internationally interwoven processes shift decision-making powers onto associations of countries such as the European Union, but also onto international organizations such as NATO and the UN, and ultimately into the arcane spaces of intergovernmental accords such as free-trade agreements. In each case there are good reasons for this. However, democratic legitimation and partic-ipation, which continues to be linked to the nation

state, suffers. Areas of human existence such as the economic system, but also environmental protection, questions about migration and energy supply are decided in various interwoven, layered, and concentric collectives. Neither theory nor political practice has thus far succeeded in releasing democratic forms of decision-making from their connection with a closed collective of citizens, traditionally known as the nation state, and in designing new democratic models for these fragmented, decision-making situations. Perhaps this is impossible. It is no accident that in the European context a large part of the rulings in the German Federal Constitutional Court in recent years has been concerned with the question of the extent to which state-centered democratic procedures and authorities may be limited according to the Basic Law [*Grundgesetz*], without abandoning core areas of statehood.[8]

2. But even in situations where national democracy can arbitrate to the fullest extent, unhindered by other actors, weakness and unwillingness to make decisions is setting in within democracy. Even in preliminary discussions, parties are finding it hard to formulate alternatives and present them to the citizen. The assertion that in many issues there are no alternative

possibilities for action paralyses debate, and is wrong and truly undemocratic. Long-term problems such as the consequences of demographic change are not tackled decisively, social security perspectives for the next fifteen years at least are not drawn up, and there is a lack of ideas concerning long-term investment in infrastructure, education, and energy supply. Here, in the national context, a solution emerges that harks back to classical models: if the parliamentary path to decision-making loses the ability to manage, then the executive takes over. Complex political decisions, which often have to be made under pressure of time, are discussed in small groups, and appear as short-term compromises that neglect long-term rationality. "One sometimes gets the impression that decisions at the political level are only possible if some kind of emergency arises; not a military emergency but rather a fiscal or budgetary emergency."[9] Perhaps most serious, however, is the decrease in citizen participation on which every democracy is existentially reliant. Voter turnout is falling, as is engagement with political groups and parties. The traditional parties are grappling with massive recruitment problems. This goes hand-in-hand with increasing individualization and differentiation in society. Above all, however, it signals a loss of confidence in the ability of the political apparatus to solve problems. In this regard it is interesting to note that, after a lack of alternatives has been proclaimed, one political party which is attracting voters with the very word "alternative" in its name and promising changes, can mobilize hitherto non-voters.[10] But our system is not set up for these two things—the role of the detached spectator or the partial, fundamental opposition—and it cannot be. It reacts by setting up more arcane executive areas with the good intention of safeguarding spaces for appropriate decision-making, but with the unfortunate consequence of disengaging politics from society.

IV.

These are all symptoms of an illness that is curable nevertheless. Crisis and continual renewal are part and parcel of democracy, otherwise it would not be a democracy. Democracy is the riskiest form of government. But democracy also involves not blowing democracy out of proportion or developing exaggerated expectations, against which any democratic practice must seem deficient.[11]

Among the suggestions for renewal the call for more citizen participation through people's initiatives, plebiscites, and referenda is taking center stage. This follows from the fact that major democratic nations are usually constituted as strictly representative democracies. Of course in Germany there exist strong elements of direct democracy at municipal and *Länder* level, but none at all where the central decisions are taken, that is at federal level. Here the Bundestag is the single constitutional organ that possesses immediate democratic legitimation based on elections by the national population. As we know, this was consciously and decisively stipulated by the fathers and mothers of the 1949 constitution, in the firm belief that the unfortunate Weimar Republic failed because of many plebiscite-related reasons. This view was already debatable. But after over 60 years of the Basic Law it should not in any way be relevant any more. Nevertheless caution should be exercised if we are to hope for a strengthening of the democratic system through more citizen participation. First, representative democracy, in which representatives make decisions on behalf of the people, is the basic form of democracies in large communities. It is not a second-class stopgap compared with idealized direct democracy, where the people vote directly on everything. Today direct democracy has a place in a functioning, representative system as its complement. Direct voting by the people is as suitable for really big decisions (membership of the EU?) as it is for local ones (a basement garage under the market square?). It depends on the possibility of delivering in a clear "yes or no" format a vote on a question, on which decision-makers, beneficiaries, and cost providers agree. It becomes problematic when the call for more direct democracy is underpinned by the implicit contrast of good, ordinary people versus bad elites. When enraged citizens talk about the "lying press," or about "those" politicians as "enemies of the people" then it becomes a top priority to win back trust in the decision-making channels of representative democracy. Their problem-solving capacity must be strengthened. Direct democracy's big moment has not arrived. It can seize upon any failures, at best intermittently. Even the new social media are little suited to extending direct democracy's range of application. Care should certainly be taken when government members and parliamentarians bring up the topic of increasing elements of direct democracy— is democracy the winner if the people vote on suggestions made by the parties and government about immigration policy?

V.

Democracy is not a land of calm and stasis. It exists only in continual movement, turbulence, and self-discovery. What it should do cannot be determined by a pre-ordained consensus, whether cultural, religious, or anything else. Authority in democracy cannot emerge from this. In a public realm democracy mediates between opinions, convictions, and interests. It is hard work and can take up a lot of time, and moreover this form of decision-making and government is more expensive than others. Democracy needs authority and it must radiate authority, but it is not allowed to be authoritarian. Its greatest threat today lies in its development into a "game without citizens,"[12] in which there is no one to give democracy authority, and where citizens do not have a sense of authority.

Notes

1. BVerfGE 77, 1. [Trans. Philippa Hurd]

2. Giovanni Sartori, *Demokratietheorie*, 1997, pp. 253 ff.

3. BVerfGE 44, 125 (142). [Trans. Philippa Hurd]

4. Ernest Renan, "Qu'est-ce qu'une Nation?," Speech given at the Sorbonne on March 11, 1882. (English translation in *Becoming National: A Reader* ed. by Geoff Eley and Ronald Grigor

Suny, trans. Martin Thom [New York and Oxford: Oxford
University Press, 1996], p. 53: "A nation's existence is, if you
will pardon the metaphor, a daily plebiscite, just as an individual's existence is a perpetual affirmation of life.")

5. Robert Piloty, *Autorität und Staatsgewalt*, 1905, p. 4:
   "Autorität als Rechtsbegriff ist [...] in der Tat von Herrschaft
   als Rechtsbegriff nicht zu unterscheiden" ["Authority as a
   legal concept cannot [...] in fact be distinguished from domination as a legal concept"].

6. Christoph Schönberger, "Autorität in der Demokratie" in
   Zeitschrift für Ideengeschichte, issue IV/4, 2010, pp. 41 ff.

7. Pertinently on this topic see Wolfgang Streeck's publications, in particular *Gekaufte Zeit* (2013); cf. also Jürgen
   Habermas, *FAZ*, 05.11.2005, p. 31.

8. BVerfGE 123, 267 – Lisbon Treaty; BVerfGE 132, 195; 135,
   317 – European Stability Mechanism.

9. Hans-Jürgen Papier, "Die Zukunft der Demokratie" in
   Festschrift für Brun-Otto Bryde, 2013, pp. 261 ff., 266.

11. Christoph Möllers, *Demokratie – Zumutungen und Versprechen*
    (Berlin: Klaus Wagenbach GmbH, 2008), p. 12: "Die
    erfolgreichsten Verächter der Demokratie idealisieren
    die Demokratie, um sie dann wegen ihres vermeintlichen
    Verrats an den eigenen Idealen zugunsten autoritärer
    Ordnungen verwerfen zu können." ["Those who are most
    successful at holding democracy in contempt idealize it in
    order to then be able to reject democracy because it has sup-
    posedly betrayed its own ideals—to the benefit of authoritar-
    ian systems."]

12. Hans Vorländer, *FAZ*, 11.07.2011.

CHAPTER 4

RESPONDING RESPONSIBLY

ROGER SCRUTON

A president or prime minister occupies an *office*, which is defined by its responsibilities; so that in every exercise of power he or she can be publicly questioned and "called to account." But the relation of accountability is not identical with that of election to office. You can obtain power by popular vote, while avoiding accountability for its exercise. You can promise things but not deliver them; you can stir up crowd emotions and then rise on the crest of them over the barrier and onto the throne, thereafter to reward only your favorites or to ignore the people entirely. In all sorts of ways voting and accountability diverge, and we have recently been made intensely aware of this by dramatic events on the stage of world politics.

In Turkey there was an attempted military coup in July 2016, followed by a massive appeal to the people by President Erdoğan, who has since arrested 3,000 judges who surely had little or nothing to do with the coup, dismissed hundreds of deans from the universities, and in general used the opportunity to advance his personal agenda, which is to replace the secular state of Kemal Atatürk with a populist Islamic democracy. Quite possibly the majority of the people support him, but what protection is he offering to those who do not? Is this the tyranny of the majority against which Mill[1] warned, and what Tocqueville[2] meant by democratic despotism? At least we want to know whether democracy, for President Erdoğan, means something more than a massive vote in his own favor—whether it is also bound up with procedures that give a voice to opposition and rights to minorities. For without those things nobody will be in a position to call Erdoğan to account. Democracy is not about voting only, but about the institutions that force politicians, even those elected by majority vote, to account for their actions.

Then again, in America, the Republican Party's candidates for nomination to the presidency were swept aside by popular vote, and an outsider who has little or no support from the experienced politicians has been elected in their stead. It is said that the political class has lost touch with the people, who are now revolting against the procedures and limitations of representative democracy and asking for a direct say in the running of their country. It is also said that we are seeing the rise of populism and demagoguery, of the kind that brought the Nazis to power. But for Donald Trump it is all very different. He says to his supporters: "The old political class, which relied on you to vote for them, did not consult your interests and behaved in Congress as though they were not accountable to you. In particular, they ignored your anxieties over immigration, national identity, and the impact of global trade. Now," Trump says, "I am giving you the opportunity to vote for someone who is accountable to you, and not to the political apparatus." Is Trump's view of the matter right?

Then we have the two enormous upheavals in the United Kingdom, with the Prime Minister, responding to growing pressure from below, promising a referendum on the UK's membership of the EU, trying and predictably failing to obtain changes to the Treaty, and then losing the vote, to his own and everyone else's surprise. Was this an example of a politician making himself accountable to the people, and paying the price? Or was politics replaced by simple majority vote, with true accountability as one of the casualties?

At the same time, thanks to changes instituted by Ed Miliband,[3] the leader of the Parliamentary Labour Party is now elected directly by the Party membership and not by the Labour Members of Parliament. As a result, the activists elect a Leader of the Opposition who does not have the trust or goodwill either of the traditional Labour voter or of those whom he must lead in Parliament, and who sits silent and impotent on the bench of the House of Commons certain only of one fact, which is that he is the elected leader. It is as though Parliament and its offices were of no interest to him; yet there is no procedure for removing him other than the one that will ensure that he is re-elected. When, a century ago, the members of the Parliamentary Conservative Party voted in a way of which their leader Bonar Law[4] disapproved, he was asked what he felt, and he replied, "I must follow them; I am their leader." The wisdom of this remark would be lost on Jeremy Corbyn.[5]

In the light of those cases we may well ask what makes an elected officer accountable, and in particular what makes him or her accountable to those who voted the other way? It is manifest that there is more to democracy than simply the rule of the majority. But what more, and how is the more shown in the workings of Parliament? The question is of importance for another and more systemic reason. Thanks to the Internet, the iPhone, and all the other gadgets that permit instant messages, crowd emotions, and Twitter storms, people can make their opinions and wishes directly known to whomever is interested, and directly influential on the legislature without passing through the political process. Politicians are besieged at all hours of the day and night by their constituents, demanding a referendum on whatever issue has not yet slipped from public memory. The referendum that has just shaken the UK is in part an official version of something that is happening all the time—the instant plebiscite, which casts aside the political process and appeals directly to the people.

Every day, petitions from Change.org or Avaaz.org pop up and one is urged to add one's voice to some current demand on behalf of the victims of this or that alleged injustice and to experience the "one click" passport to moral virtue. It is not that the causes are wrong: without the kind of extensive debate that it is the duty of a parliament to conduct it is hard to decide on their merits. Nevertheless, one is being asked to add one's vote in the absence of any institution that will hold anyone to account for the result. Nobody is asking us, the people, to think the matter through, or to raise the question of what other interests need to be considered, besides the one mentioned in the petition. Nobody in this process, neither the ones who propose the petitions nor the many who sign them, have the responsibility of getting things right or run the risk of being ejected from office if they fail to do so. The background conditions of representative government have simply been thought away, and all we have is the mass expression of opinion, without responsibility or risk. Not a single person who signs the petition, including those who compose it, will bear the full cost of it. For the cost is transferred to everyone, on behalf of whatever single-issue pressure group takes the benefit.

The history of parliaments in Europe is the history of representation, in which the various important interests in the state have been represented before the sovereign, whose decisions depended on their consent. Rousseau[6] famously objected to representative government as a denial of the free choice of the people, whose "general will" emerges only if all of them participate in the important decisions. But he had no clear idea how to govern a large modern society by direct appeal to the people. Now, with everyone armed with a smartphone, it might be said that Rousseau's ideal is within our reach. And the result is not just Donald Trump, Jeremy Corbyn, and Brexit, but a constant rain of petitions touching on everything that happens to be briefly in the news.

In his famous speech to the electors of Bristol, whom he was persuading to vote for him as their Member of Parliament, Edmund Burke[7] distinguished between a representative, which is what he hoped to be, and a delegate. A delegate is someone chosen by a group of people to relay their opinion or their decision. The responsibility of the delegate begins and ends with the announcement of a decision already made by others. In other words, the delegate makes no decision of his own, and therefore no decision for which he is accountable. If politicians were delegates, they would never be in the position to say "be it on my own head what I now decide." They would be the mere instruments for decisions and opinions that they cannot change and which they might even disown.

Representatives, Burke argued, are not like that at all. They are not elected to relay the opinions of their constituents; they are elected to represent their constituents' interests. They must make decisions according to their own conscience, regardless of whether their constituents happen to agree with them. That is what it means, to take responsibility.

Burke put the matter in a much-quoted passage that deserves to be quoted again:

> ...It ought to be the happiness and glory of a representative to live in the strictest union, the closest correspondence, and the most unreserved communication with his constituents. Their wishes ought to have great weight with him; their opinion, high respect; their business, unremitted attention. It is his duty to sacrifice his repose, his pleasures, his satisfactions, to theirs; and above all, ever, and in all cases, to prefer their interest to his own. But his un-biased opinion, his mature judgment, his enlightened conscience, he ought not to sacrifice to you, to any man, or to any set of men living. These he does not derive from your pleasure; no, nor from the law and the constitution. They are a trust from Providence, for the abuse of which he is deeply answerable. Your representative owes you, not his industry only, but his judgment; and he betrays, instead of serving you, if he sacrifices it to your opinion.[8]

For representative government to work, representatives must be free to ignore the petitions of those who elected them, to consider each matter on its merits, and to address the interests of those who did not vote for them just as much as the interests of those who did. The important point is that representation, unlike delegation, is an *office*, defined by its responsibilities. To refer every matter to the constituents and to act on majority opinion case by case is precisely to avoid those responsibilities, to retreat behind the consensus, and to cease to be genuinely accountable for what one does.

That illustrates another important idea, which is the connection between accountability and authority. A representative is *authorize* by the constituents to take decisions on their behalf: and their authorizing the representative in this way is what makes the representative accountable to them. Representatives therefore have the *authority* to take decisions in the assembly, and not just the power. *Power* is legitimate only when exercised by the one who is *authorize* to do so. Authority can be conferred from above by a person or institution that already possesses it, as when Parliament *authorizes* an officer to act on its behalf. But how is authority conferred on the one who authorizes? Surely not from above but from below, either by the voters or by the traditions and institutions that encapsulate their long-term interests and shared identity.

This conferring of authority may be by election or by the assumption of an historical office according to the requirements of law (as in the case of a monarch). But there is no office without the responsibilities that define it, and to exercise power outside the limits set by those responsibilities is to act, as the law puts it, *ultra vires*—beyond the powers conferred. That view of the political process is subversive of the Marxist tradition. It tells us that politics is not about power but about authority, and that authority comes when people are accountable, directly or indirectly, to others who have less power than themselves.

Parliaments are subject to complex procedures, committees, and reviews. They exist in order to inject hesitation and circumspection into the legislative process. They can get things wrong, they can become corrupt and dictatorial; they may be so much concerned with majority opinion as to neglect minorities. But their purpose is to represent the nation as a whole, and to take decisions in which all the competing interests are consulted and, so far as possible, reconciled. Of course, it would be a foolish Member of Parliament who decided to ignore public opinion, and in this respect we must recognize that the new social media have to a certain extent made politicians more aware of what people think. But public opinion is not a monopoly of those who strive their utmost to mobilize it. The silent, the hesitant, and the deferential have opinions too, and there may be a lot more of them than there are of the vociferous crowds who capture the attention of the media. Moreover, what people think is not necessarily what they say they think. Public opinion in a democracy is not a matter of the preparedness to say "yes" or "no" to some simplified question posed on a website. It is the result of a process, in which fleeting whims are filtered out from real concerns, and the underlying motivations of people are revealed not just to the rest of us, but to the people themselves. We become aware of what we really think only through dialogue and disagreement, and not through blurting out what comes momentarily to the front of consciousness, or through responding to questions designed to elicit a "yes" or a "no."

In other words, public opinion *emerges* from the broad currents of argument and reflection among people who are ready at any moment to defer to the facts and to acknowledge the right of others to disagree with their judgment. It is precisely through such institutions as parliament that public opinion finds its voice. We are not creatures of the moment; we do not necessarily know what our own interests are, but depend upon advice and discussion. Hence we need processes that impede us from making impetuous choices, and which bring us face-to-face with our real interests. It is precisely this that is being obscured by the emerging "plebiscite culture." Decisions are being made at the point of least responsibility, by the man or woman in the street with an iPhone, asked suddenly to click "yes" or "no" in response to an issue that they have never thought about before and may never think about again.

So what, now, of referenda? Are these, too, examples of the plebiscite culture, in which decisions bypass all the institutions that would inject the needed measure of accountability into the minds of those who make them? Are political leaders who call a referendum renouncing their responsibility in the matter, and handing over to those who equally have no responsibility, since they pay no personal cost for their mistakes? The United Kingdom, which has rarely had a referendum on anything, has recently had two in a row, one on Scotland's membership of the UK, and one on the UK's membership of the European Union. And in each case it seemed that only a referendum could answer the question being considered, since it was not a question of policy but a question of identity—a question concerning who we, the people, really are.

Many prefer not to raise such questions, so deep and intractable are the emotions that attach to them. In modern conditions, in which governments rarely enjoy a majority vote, most of us are living under a government of which we don't approve. We accept to be ruled by laws and decisions made by politicians with whom we disagree, and whom we perhaps deeply dislike. How is that possible? Why don't democracies constantly collapse, as people refuse to be governed by those they never voted for? The answer is that democracies are held together by something stronger than politics. There is a "first person plural," a pre-political loyalty, which causes neighbors who voted in opposing ways to treat each other as fellow citizens, for whom the government is not "mine" or "yours" but "ours," whether or not we approve of it. Many are the flaws in this system of government, but one feature gives it an insuperable advantage over all others so far devised, which is that it makes all those who exercise power accountable to those who did not vote for them—something that President Erdoğan cannot deal with. This kind of accountability is possible only if the electorate is bound together as a "we." Only if this "we" is in place can the people trust the politicians to look after their interests, whether or not they have their vote. When that trust is in place people can cooperate in ensuring that the legislative process is reversible, when it makes a mistake.

The institutions of the European Union stand, however, in another relation to us. The Commission is not elected and its legislation is not openly discussed. There is no organized opposition, and no clear procedure for correcting mistakes or for ejecting those who make them. And there is no way of rectifying these defects since there is no "we" who can insist on another arrangement. All that we the people can do is to get our governments to amend or withdraw from the Treaty.

In a parliamentary democracy legislation changes, and constitutions evolve, according to the will of the people. But when legislation is controlled by a Treaty, and the Treaty itself can be changed only by majority vote of the signatories, the legislative process stagnates, proceeding with an agenda that has never adapted to the changed conditions of Europe, and which cannot adapt to them now. We have seen this in connection with what, for the British people, is the most critical feature of the Treaty of Rome, namely that providing for freedom of movement within the Union, which has stimulated an unprecedented tide of immigration into their country, which they have no legal power to limit. Nobody foresaw the effect of this provision when the original Treaty was signed; but nobody can undo the provision just because it is leading to what, for the ordinary person, is a demographic catastrophe. We must go on following the instructions, even though they were written in another world, by people long since dead.

That was the issue that led to the referendum. Parliament could not discuss or amend the Treaty, and those elected to Parliament had to confess that, in a matter of great concern to those who voted for them, they were not accountable, since Parliament had no say in the matter. A breakdown in the system of accountability had occurred, and there was no remedy to this. All that could be done was to ask the people whether they could live with it. And they said no. The result has caused great bitterness and division within the country. Many who feel bound to accept the decisions of a government, even though they did not vote for it and even though only a small minority of people voted for it, have declared themselves unwilling to accept the result of the referendum. And this is surely proof of the fact that, for us, democracy is *not* about majority voting, but about accountability, and that all direct appeals to the people put accountability at risk. Just where we go from here is, of course, another matter. But at least the problem has been handed back to our representatives in Parliament, and we, the people, can pass the buck to them.

Notes

1. John Stuart Mill (1806–73), British philosopher and economist, one of the most influential liberal thinkers of the 19th century. Proponent of utilitarianism, considered to be a social reformer.

2. Alexis de Tocqueville (1805–59), French publicist, politician, and historian. He is considered to be the pioneer of comparative politics.

3. Edward Samuel "Ed" Miliband (1969–), British politician. MP since 2005; Leader of the Labour Party and Leader of the Opposition 2010–15.

4. Andrew Bonar Law (1858–1923), British politician of the Conservative Party; Prime Minister 1922–23.

5. Jeremy Bernard Corbyn (1949–), British politician of the Labour Party. Was elected Labour Leader after Ed Miliband's resignation in September 2015.

6. Jean-Jacques Rousseau (1712–78), Francophone Genevan writer, philosopher, educator, and naturalist during the Enlightenment.

7. Edmund Burke (1729–97), Anglo-Irish writer, philosopher, and politician during the Enlightenment. Considered the philosophical founder of modern Conservatism.

8. Edmund Burke, Speech to the Electors of Bristol, 1774.

CHAPTER 5

AUTHORITY IN THE MEDIA INDUSTRY

KAI A. KONRAD[1]

On June 23, 2016 the majority of voters in the United Kingdom elected to leave the European Union. Following this decision numerous authorities have offered their opinion, many of which have assumed that this decision will have clearly negative consequences for the British economy and science. Many journalists have taken up these hypotheses, emphasizing and repeating them. For example, Nina Trentmann and Thomas Heuzeroth wrote in *Die Welt* online on June 24: "It is expected that not only the British finance industry but also the entire British economy will shrink considerably."[2] On June 24 Carsten Herz wrote in *Handelsblatt*: "Now, within two years, between 500,000 and 800,000 jobs could be lost, as emerged in one study produced by Chancellor George Osborne before the vote. According to this study the country would enter a recession and the pound would drop in value considerably."[3] *Die Zeit* online reported on June 26: "The US rating agency Moody's anticipates a decline in consumer spending and investments, and thus slower economic growth in Great Britain. The agency said that the outlook had been lowered from 'stable' to 'negative'."[4] In *Handelsblatt* on June 27 Katharina Slodczyk wrote: "Secondly, Brexit will aggravate these wounds even more, and plunge the country into an economic crisis—possibly even into recession."[5] On the same day Bettina Schulz wrote in *Die Zeit* online: "At the moment it looks worse. If politicians cannot agree even in the long term, neither within Great Britain, nor with the EU, then uncertainty could increase. Consumers could take fright and Great Britain slide into recession."[6] On June 28 Jens Münchrath and Jan Hildebrand wrote in *Handelsblatt*: "In the case of Brexit, of course, the British economy would in all probability be more negatively affected than continental Europe. In this case economists such as ifo president Clemens Fuest anticipate an 'adjustment recession'."[7]

These opinions are a small selection. I cannot exclude the possibility of isolated instances of positive comment in the German press, although I cannot recall any.

Nevertheless, this rather clear and negative collection of opinions presents an interesting phenomenon. A country's economic development is determined overwhelmingly, in both the mid- and long-term, by fundamental factors. Economic studies suggest that institutional and cultural factors are significantly responsible for whether a country develops economic power and increases in growth and prosperity. Among the significant, positive regulatory conditions are efficient markets and forms of commodity exchange that are transparent and as free as possible from barriers to access, as well as a legal system that clearly and transparently separates the property rights of the individual from other private individuals and from state institutions, and enforces these property rights in a simple, quick, reliable, and cost-effective way.

In this respect Great Britain is not badly off. Every year, in its "Competitiveness Index" the World Economic Forum produces a country ranking. The index attempts to condense the various institutional components that define a country's competitiveness into a measured value that can then be compared with other countries. This index gives the UK an excellent report.[8] In the 2015–16 index, of all surveyed nations, the UK occupies tenth place in the overall ranking. In some subsections, the UK performs considerably better: under the criterion of "Technological Readiness" the UK is in third place behind Luxembourg and Switzerland.

With its "Index of Economic Freedom" the Heritage Foundation also regularly produces a country ranking. The index is based on various sub-indices: rule of law, limited government, regulatory efficiency, and freedom or openness of markets. In Europe the UK is ranked fourth (behind Switzerland, Ireland, and Estonia), and globally comes in at tenth place.[9] It is interesting that of the five leaders in this ranking Hong Kong, Singapore, New Zealand, and Australia represent four former colonies, that is states whose cultural and institutional foundations were shaped significantly by the UK.

Of course in the short term, it is often other factors that determine a country's economic development. One of these factors is psychology. Economic development frequently requires similar or complementary actions to be taken by many economic actors. Consequently, trust in the actions of others, and with it trust in economic recovery or the stability of the economic climate play a decisive role. In this situation the authority of the press comes into the frame.

The reports and predictions of the UK's economic decline, if they are delivered as predictions with sufficient authority, take on a life of their own. The forecasts themselves can even in the short term lead all too easily to the fulfillment of these same forecasts. To this extent it is noteworthy that the negative press has as yet not led to a massive economic collapse in the UK. Nevertheless, in its latest annual report for 2016/17,[10] the German Council of Economic Experts states: "In the case of Brexit negative economic effects are to be expected first of all. In the short-term, however, these may be moderate" (see Chapter 4, section 288).

These observations give rise to a discussion of the concept of authority in the media industry and its dangers. Generally speaking, the authority of an expert is expressed in the fact that one trusts what he says, because he possesses superior knowledge. The greater his authority, the less the expert is required to justify his statements through argument or by producing data or background information. An expert who does not as yet have much authority, will usually have to prove his propositions, for example by means of theoretical observations or empirical findings. A major authority, on the other hand, can make a statement of fact or prediction without providing proof. The mechanics of reputation are in the main the basis on which expert authority is developed. And if many experts make statements independently of one another, a clear picture may be formed from the aggregation of this information. However, information economics tells us that the mechanisms for aggregating expert information do not always produce a beneficial effect. An important cause of this lies in different forms of herd behavior.

For example, for reputational reasons an expert may have an incentive not to differ from the opinion of his expert colleagues in forming his own opinion. He who agrees with the expert opinion of all his colleagues when making his predictions about a topic has little to lose. Even if the prediction later turns out to be completely wrong, the loss of reputation is not particularly great: the expert can rightly point out that almost all his colleagues arrived at the same prediction. If this expert had adopted a minority position and offered a different prediction, this would have been a risky game. If this prediction had not come true, the expert would have gambled away most of his reputation.

Authors such as Banerjee[11] and Bikhchandani, Hirshleifer, and Welch[12] have pointed persuasively to another problem. They show that the sequential forecasts or decisions of experts can lead to a situation where the total amount of knowledge and information available to all experts does not even come close to aggregating an effective overall picture. Precisely when the issue for experts is not being wrong in their own forecasts, this can lead to statements where all those involved produce a completely unanimous judgment that is actually completely incorrect and misleading in light of the basic information available.

This seemingly paradoxical outcome can be illustrated using the following example of an information cascade focusing on judgments made by journalists and commentators in the media. Our example imagines a media industry comprising dominant media and media that report stories subsequently. The situation has been idealized such that the various newspapers offering a prediction or opinion about a topic do so in sequence. Newspaper 1 begins, then newspaper 2 and so on, until finally the free sheets take up the story. The story to be reported, let us imagine, is a prediction about the consequences of Brexit, on whether this is good or bad for Great Britain's economic development.

The dominant media outlet may have access to somewhat better sources of information than the subsequent newspaper 2, and so on, and the sources of information are at least partially independent from each other.

In this case we could simply let the newspapers agree with each other simultaneously and anonymously, for example on the advantageousness of Brexit for Great Britain. For a sufficiently large number of newspapers the view of the majority would really be the correct answer, even with near certain probability. This is the lesson of Condorcet's jury theorem, a statistical insight that is now over 200 years old and originates with the scholar and probability theorist the Marquis de Condorcet, being named for him.

In the publication process described above, however, information is aggregated in a way that is different from the process of majority voting. The reporter at newspaper 1 must say whether he thinks Brexit is good or bad for Great Britain before he knows what information his colleagues have. He delivers a prediction that corresponds to his level of information, even if his level of information could be relatively low compared with the total amount of information available to all newspapers.

The prediction might say that Brexit will be rather bad for the UK. Now newspaper 2 comes into play. The editors possess two kinds of information: on the one hand they have their own sources, and on the other they can see that newspaper 1's view is that Brexit is bad for the UK. If newspaper 1's information is just as valid as newspaper 2's, then the editors of newspaper 2 should no longer trust their own information but follow the decision of their colleagues in newspaper 1 and join them in writing that Brexit is bad for the UK.

This is the critical moment for an incipient information cascade. The editors of newspaper 2 cast their own sources to the winds, because what they learn from newspaper 1's report carries more weight than their own sources. At this point in the opinion-forming process newspaper 2's information is forgotten.

Now two newspapers have already written that Brexit is bad for the UK. The information cascade has begun and cannot be stopped unless there is an editor whose own information is so robust that it counts for more than the information coming from all previous reports. If this is not the case, the information cascade continues until finally even the free sheets agree with the opinion expressed in newspaper 1.

This outcome occurs even if all editors with the exception of newspaper 1 actually do have private information that suggests instead that Brexit is advantageous for the UK. If all those involved had put their various sources of information on the table before writing their articles, and had come to a joint verdict on this basis, they would have reached a completely different opinion. However, this is how an information cascade works, in which everyone formed his own opinion completely rationally, but as a whole the reporting did not adequately reflect the information available.

Herd behavior[13] can also lead to a situation where the media industry, despite its plurality and without malicious intent, no longer reflects the whole diversity of opinion in an appropriate way, and only shines a light on a fraction of all available information.

The problem intensifies when, in an increasingly difficult media market, the financial margins for research and information-gathering are shrinking. Thus even the piece of information that determines the opinion of the dominant media outlet is often not particularly robust, but is nevertheless adopted by subsequent media because of their even weaker level of knowledge.

It is said that the problem of the information cascade was tackled by the Prussian General Staff using one simple rule. When a status report was required, the opinion of the youngest member with the least authority was sought first of all, then that of the second-youngest member, and so on. In this way it was possible to avert an information cascade of the type described above. The person whose opinion was asked had at the time of asking not yet heard the expertise of a person with greater authority. They could thus contribute their information in an unbiased way, instead of simply following the opinion of older members of the General Staff.

We should remember that this demonstration of information cascades using the example of Brexit is purely hypothetical. It illustrates one possibility. Whether the negative press on the Brexit result described above was the result of an information cascade cannot be answered here. However, this example points to the possible dangers of trusting the authority of the media.

Notes

1. I am grateful to Niklas Gebhard for research assistance. Academic responsibility for the contents of this article remains with the author.

2. Nina Trentmann and Thomas Heuzeroth, 24.06.2016, "Das sind die Folgen des britischen EU-Ausstiegs" in *Die Welt* online, https://www.welt.de/wirtschaft/article156519802/ Das-sind-die-Folgen-des-britischen-EU-Ausstiegs.html (accessed on 16.11.2016, 11:48). English translation of press reports in notes 2–7 by Philippa Hurd.

3. Herz, Carsten, 24.06.2016, "Brexit-Folgen, Eine Bremsspur in Tiefrot" in *Handelsblatt* online, http://www.handelsblatt. com/unternehmen/industrie/brexit-folgen-eine-bremsspur-in-tiefrot/13782690.html (accessed on 16.11.2016, 12:27.)

4. Dpa, O.V., 26.06.2016, "Studie: Britische Wirtschaft großer Brexit-Verlierer" in *Die Zeit* online, http://www.zeit.de/news/2016-06/26/eu-studie-britische-wirtschaft-grosser-brexit-verlierer-26144405 (accessed on 10.11.2016.)

5. Slodczyk, Katharina, 27.06.2016 "Mit Schwung in den Abgrund" in *Handelsblatt,* no. 121, p. 10.

6. Schulz, Bettina, 27.06.2016, "Die Angst der Banker vor dem Brexit" in *Die Zeit* online, http://www.zeit.de/wirtschaft/2016-06/london-banken-brexit-folgen-arbeitsmarkt-finanzmarkt (accessed on 10.11.2016.)

7. Jens Münchrath and Jan Hildebrand, 28.06.2016, "Unverzichtbare Nation" in *Handelsblatt,* no. 122, p. 10.

8. Cf. World Economic Forum, 2015, *Global Competitiveness Report 2015,* http://reports.weforum.org/global-competitiveness-report-2015-2016/economies/#indexId=GCI&economy=GBR (accessed on 03.11.2016.)

9. Cf. Heritage Foundation, 2016, *2016 Index of Economic Freedom – Country Rankings,* http://www.heritage.org/index/ranking.aspx?nomobile (accessed on 03.11.2016.)

10. Cf. SVR, 2016, *Jahresgutachten 2016/17 – Zeit für Reformen,* http://www.sachverstaendigenrat-wirtschaft.de/fileadmin/dateiablage/gutachten/jg201617/ges_jg16_17.pdf (accessed on 03.11.2016.) English version: German Council of Economic Experts, *Annual Report 2016/17 – Time for Reforms,* https://www.sachverstaendigenrat-wirtschaft.de/jahresgutachten-2016-2017.html?&L=1 (accessed on 23.12.16.)

11. Abhijit V. Banerjee, "A Simple Model of Herd Behavior" in *Quarterly Journal of Economics* 107(3), (1992), pp. 797–817.

12. Sushil Bikhchandani, David Hirshleifer, and Ivo Welch, "A Theory of Fads, Fashion, Custom, and Cultural Change as Informational Cascades" in *Journal of Political Economy,* 100(5), (1992), pp. 992–1026.

13. As formally described and analyzed in an abstract context by Abhijit V. Banerjee, and by Sushil Bikhchandani, David Hirshleifer, and Ivo Welch, see notes 11 and 12.

CHAPTER 6

DOES THE LAW STILL HAVE AUTHORITY?

CHRISTOPH G. PAULUS

The answer to this question seems clear if we think about the almost hymn-like praises heaped upon today's dominant supremacy of the law. In such paeans the monarch has been replaced by the law, and even the European Union is praised as a community of law and in law. Compared with earlier times, this estimation is completely understandable, although insofar as it seems to imply a development, it suppresses the danger of the status quo we have now reached. Indeed, it is not incontrovertibly the case that where we are now might represent, unchallenged, the starting point for advancement along this route. As we have had to recognize again and again in recent times that something as apparently obvious as democracy requires continual vigilance and nurturing and in no way means an irreversible achievement, in the area of the law too we must give ongoing attention and awareness to making sure that what has been achieved is maintained and advanced.

The following observations are dedicated to this commandment; they contain a warning—or indeed a call for increased vigilance.

I. STARTING POINT

In order to be able to answer the question about the authority of the law, we must first define what authority means, and then consider whether the law has ever had authority.

To simplify matters let us accept first of all that authority is an emanation that is recognized and accepted in and for itself and requires no further authorization. This admittedly rather superficial definition, when applied to the law, implies that in order to have authority it must be applied or obeyed, *because* it is the law. Of course this must not degenerate into an end in itself. History (Germany's in particular) is full of serious and terrible examples of legal authority that has been exercised unjustly and improperly. Aristotle early on saw the necessity of correcting the severity of the law through *epieikeia*—and became, via Cicero's Latin translation of this concept as *aequitas*, the inventor of what has been established in English Common Law as a corrective value for many centuries, namely equity. However, once the law has passed through the filter of justice, of fundamental rights, etc., it must be applied, *because* it is law.

Answering the other preliminary question—has the law ever had authority?—depends on what we understand by "ever." At this point we could delve deep into legal history and trace the highs and lows of the law's struggle for precedence. We could go back to the time when the law replaced customs and traditions, thereby implicitly indicating that the value system of that period had changed. A significant example of this during the first century BCE in Ancient Rome is the emergence of the right to a compulsory portion. In the chaos of civil war, the tradition of naming one's own descendants as heirs had apparently disappeared. In order to counter this decline in family cohesion a law re-introduced this tradition by exerting pressure to declare a testator, who had not named his descendants as heirs in his will, as mentally ill at the time of writing the will. The consequence of this (so-called *querela inofficiosi testamenti*) was that his will became null and void, and the inheritance was forthwith distributed appropriately among the legal heirs, among whom the primary heirs were the descendants.

But we could also locate this "ever" earlier still in history, and even during times when the law played a considerably smaller role than it does now, encounter the dichotomy—which is still relevant today—of the law as a regulating mechanism on the one hand and as an instrument of power on the other. Yet further back in history we would probably have to end our investigations at the point when we might ask how, at a certain point in human development, a commitment acquired a legally binding character. What resulted much later in the principle of *pacta sunt servanta*—for example, the promise to hand over 50 hundredweight of next summer's harvest—must have begun at a particular point, and thus must have acquired an early form of legal authority. The question that of course ensues from this inquiry, namely what is the difference between such a (legal) offer and the commitment (which is considered non-binding) to take part in this year's Convoco Forum,[1] is still not really explained.

But even if we understand the above-mentioned "ever" not as a historical reference but as referring to the present, we discover numerous signs indicating that the law clearly has authority. Even as pedestrians we stop when the stoplight shows red. We take the utmost notice of the rulings of the German Federal Constitutional Court or of the European Court of Justice. The European Union is founded on law and is controlled by the law and its seemingly limitless emanations. Currently there is one regulation that concerns us greatly: Article 50 of the Lisbon Treaty (TEU)—that is the notice of withdrawal from the EU— has become a kind of key to the future of our continent, for our togetherness, and probably also for the continuation of the unique period of peace which we have all had the immense privilege of enjoying over the past 70 years in Western Europe.

What other authority is comparable to this? After all, these fundamentally important future developments are dependent on our satisfying a process that is established by a legislative act. As a result of this and because of the above observations, the question raised by the title of this essay can initially be answered in the positive: yes, laws still have authority.

II. DOUBTS

On closer examination, however, this monumental block of authority shows signs of erosion. Let us begin with a phenomenon that may come up in our modern life: online trading. Amazon and other retailers are capturing the markets for anything from books to islands, from food to shoes—it can all be ordered online and delivered to our doors in double-quick time. Depending on the purchased item and location— Germany for example is a notoriously problematic market for Internet retailers—50 percent of orders and more are returned. As consumer protection allows the right of return to apply to online trading, the average customer tends to ignore its restriction to this kind of sale, and claims the right of return even in the case of purchases made in a city store. In order to survive in the massive competition with online stores, these stores are well advised—regardless of their legal position to the contrary—to take back goods that have already been sold and to refund the purchase price.

What does this now mean with regard to the apparently fundamental principle of *pacta sunt servanta*? Not only that contracts can be seen less and less as permanently binding, but also that the costs of such transactions are rising dramatically; delivery to the customer and back again has a price that must be borne by the seller. In such situations, business calculations are becoming increasingly difficult and this encourages a concentration of businesses. Only the strongest survive, for example by setting up the infrastructure by which they can earn money on every product dispatched.

A similar discrepancy between "law in the books" and "law in action" is evident in the world of economics. Company departments responsible for compliance are becoming bigger and bigger. They must guarantee that a company operates in accordance with the law—no easy task given the huge and constantly growing number of existing regulations in Germany alone. The task grows if the company must also comply with European regulations, and it grows in earnest if the laws of non-EU states, such as Japan, Brazil, or Egypt, must be also implemented and taken into account.

However, there is reason to fear that the emergence of compliance involves more than just the attempt to cope with quantities. By its very existence, compliance divides the law into two components: law-making on the one hand, and legal compliance on the other. What was once a unity—the law had to be obeyed once it existed—is today a two-stage process: the enactment of a law is separate from its subsequent application.

And it is precisely from this that the above-mentioned erosion in the monolithic authority of the law could potentially result.

It should be noted that in this I am not broaching the issues of infringements or breaches of the law; these have a long tradition both in the case of rulers and the ruled. Prussian king Frederick the Great's famous intervention in the trial against Arnold the miller around 250 years ago is like George W. Bush's declaration before the Iraq invasion, namely that he couldn't care less what the international law experts said—examples that stand for millions of other cases of breaches of the law.

Rather, what is meant here is what Stefan Korioth appositely called the more and more frequently observable phenomenon of "symbolic legislation."[2] By this we mean law-making that is intended to satisfy the current needs and demands of the general public, but about which it is clear at the time of its enactment that it is only intended to be applied when this appears appropriate. A topical and particularly salient example of this from recent times is the bailout prohibition in the Treaty on the Functioning of the European Union (TFEU). Even if at the time of its enactment this prohibition was to be understood as absolutely applicable, by spring 2010 this understanding was

obsolete. Contrary to the venerable rule of interpretation according to which it is not the wording
but the intention of a treaty that should prevail, the
bailout was initiated. A few years previously another
circumvention of the law took place, not by means of
interpretation but through the alteration of existing
regulations: this was, for example, when Germany
was among the first Member States to contravene the
Treaty's stability requirements. And Christine Lagarde
made this disposability of the law wonderfully clear
when she said on the subject of the Greek financial
crisis: "Forget about the Treaty."

In the second half of 2016 another example of
symbolic legislation became public. It concerns Italy's
rescue of the Monte dei Paschi di Siena bank, among
others. After the collapse of Lehman Brothers everyone
said that there would be no more bank rescues via
bailout, and tax revenues should no longer be squan-
dered on bank rescue packages. The new miracle word
was "bail-in," in which owners should have to bear
the burden of bankruptcy. On reflection, of course,
this was no new invention: rather, this just reaffirmed
that the general rules of conventional market activity
should also apply to financial institutions: the entre-
preneur can make the most of the opportunities and in
return they must bear the risk. This model was used in

the case of Cyprus where, in the form of the so-called Recovery and Resolution Directive, European legislation enacted an enormously complicated and confusing law. Broadly speaking, this model makes available instruments through which financial institutions can be saved or resolved—including with the aid of a cascade of bail-ins. In order to save taxpayers' money, a worst-case fund should even be set up, in case the bail-in alone turns out to be insufficient.

In the case of Italy, of course, we are confronted with an instance where a gigantic debt mountain of 360 billion euros is at stake—a sum that goes beyond the capacities of any fund, even if the latter is combined with some kind of bail-in. Once again this takes us back to the well-known concept of "too big to fail," as the result of which an ultimate exception is made, and all previous agreements and promises are obsolete.

Article 32(4)(d)(iii) of the abovementioned directive permits a deviation from the general strategy if there is the danger of serious disruption in a Member State's economy. And it is precisely to this that Italy makes reference with its establishment of a national fund to rescue four central Italian banks, including Monte dei Paschi di Siena. The first application of the directive is immediately labelled an exception. Banks that have not passed the so-called stress test will be kept afloat regardless of the obvious necessity of their closure. And the reason for this lies in the everyday fact that to a certain extent politics has donned a straitjacket: the Italian President has linked his destiny to the success or failure of a referendum which has not the least connection with the banking crisis of the past.[3] In other words, the exception is used to pave the way for a vote on the political future of the President to be held at a later time.

A first, albeit superficial, conclusion to be drawn from this could be that the law, independent of any symbolism in legislation, still seems to have authority, since the attempt at bank bailout is based on a particular article in a particular directive. But on closer inspection, it is clear that the law is formulated in such a way that it can also be applied contrary to the originally formulated aim. While the law should be understood as an imperative and a principle for all future cases, politics adapts to the needs and requirements of the day. This antagonism between law and politics is undermined when laws are formulated in such a way that an action operating against the proclaimed intention is possible; for in this way the law orients itself according to the requirements of politics and with it, is in danger of losing its authority. At the same time, it is thereby deprived of one of its most valuable characteristics, namely its ability to anticipate certain outcomes.

Under these circumstances it seems to be an absolute blessing that no legal solution has thus far been found in the context of sovereign bankruptcy, that is, no proposed legislation has as yet been accepted. Currently each solution emerges as an ad hoc decision, and thus the dramatic situation, which is a present reality not only in Greece and Argentina but in dozens of other countries, avoids any predictability. Nevertheless, proposals have been made—from comprehensive insolvency processes via diluted procedures to simple netting agreements in order to reduce the unimaginably large debt mountains. Politics, however, shies away from adopting these measures, possibly because they do not guarantee the flexibility desired when setting the political agenda.

III. WARNING

Of course the examples we have chosen represent only a very small part of the wider area of danger. Nevertheless, they show with sufficient clarity that this is in no way a question of marginalia, but of legal essentials such as *pacta sunt servanta* or the reliability of political programmes enacted as law. Thus care is necessary, as the greatest guarantee of individual freedom is still linked to the rule of law. This foundation must be preserved.

Notes

1. 2016 Convoco Forum: "Authority in Question," July 30, 2016, Salzburg. http://www.convoco.co.uk/archive/events/10

2. Prof. Dr. Stefan Korioth, Professor of Public Law and Ecclesiastical Law at Ludwig Maximilian University, Munich, coined this term during discussions at the 2012 Convoco Forum.

3. At the time of writing, the repercussions of the referendum of December 4, 2016, on comprehensive constitutional changes were still unknown. A majority rejected the proposal, and the Prime Minister Matteo Renzi resigned. The said law could, thus, easily have been applied.

CHAPTER 7

THE AUTHORITY OF THE LAW IN FLUX

PETER M. HUBER

I. POLITICS CONTAINED BY LAW AS GERMANY'S CONTRIBUTION TO THE WESTERN-STYLE CONSTITUTIONAL STATE

Unconditional respect for the authority of the law is part of Germany's national identity. It has grown up over centuries and has led to a wide variety of "entries in our collective dictionary."

1. If we look at the root causes of the tendency to contain politics, which is particularly pronounced in the German culture, we see that, unlike their neighbors among the emerging Western nation states, the Germans found that the complex political governance of the Holy Roman Empire of the German Nation could only be managed to some extent through the law, and that courts (the Imperial Chamber Court [1495], for example, or the Aulic Council [1497/98]) were important guarantors in the enforcement of interests. The legend of the Miller of Sanssouci and the phrase attributed to him, "il y a des juges à Berlin", or key provisions of the 1794 General State Laws for the Prussian States such as the principle of proportionality (Section 10 II 17 PrALR) and the establishment of statutes for compensation claims in the case of state seizures of an individual's legal assets (Sections 74, 75 Introduction PrALR) are still current today. They were based on the judicial containment and moderation of the monarchical executive which was remarkable for its time. Only in this context could Immanuel Kant write at the end of the 18th century: "Law must never be accommodated to politics, but politics always accommodated to law."

The elevated status of the law also had an impact on the 19th century, as it was the instrument through which the "historic compromise" between the monarchic and the democratic principles could be brought about after the failed 1848 Revolution. It was this that bestowed on Germany the state under the rule of law in its formal or specifically statist version. The principles of the precedence of law and subjection to the law not only contained the monarchical executive in terms of the principle of legality but also guaranteed extensive personal freedoms to citizens as a (partial) functional equivalent of democracy. The task of administrative law was to dam up, in Otto Mayer's phrase "the flooding mass of administrative activity," just as the task of the gradually emerging administrative courts was to operationalize the laws of the state under the rule of law.

The National Socialist dictatorship betrayed this legacy as well. A legal system in which the will of the Führer was the highest law—even if there may have been special cases in the Nazi state, as in every dictatorship—was structurally not in a position to fulfill the task inherent to the law according to this German tradition in particular, namely to contain politics and to limit its scope of action in the interests of freedom and equality.

2. After the postwar liberation, however, work began in earnest on the reestablishment, consolidation, and fine-tuning of the state under the rule of law. The years following 1949 are characterized by the development of a constitutional jurisdiction, a comprehensive constitutionalization of the legal system, and a fine-tuning of judicial safeguards. In this respect they seem to be the logical continuation and fulfillment of the journey that had been started in the 19th century. The public law of the "old" Federal Republic, the Federal Constitutional Court, the constitutional law professors at that time, in particular Ernst Wolfgang Böckenförde, Konrad Hesse, and Peter Lerche, as well as experts in civil law such as Claus Wilhelm Canaris, concentrated their energies on the increasingly elaborate development of the Basic Law, on the constitutionalization of the (non-constitutional) legal system, and on a continual expansion of individual, public rights. Few doubts were expressed about this development. Complaints about an inordinate growth of the state under the rule of law and a lack of international compatibility in the German concept of the Basic Law, as well as warnings against a "gouvernement des juges"—against a state under the sway of judges and the law—emerged only towards the end of the 1980s.

3. In other words, politics in Germany has always been not only a democratic tussle for political majorities but also about problem-solving using the law and the courts. However, this accent on a regulation-oriented understanding of (public) law that limits politics forces legislation into the role of structural opposition to the ruling majorities. It is not by chance that the protection of fundamental rights is understood as the protection of minorities. Even the Federal Constitutional Court's proceedings on the Maastricht Treaty, the launch of the Euro, the Lisbon Treaty, aid for Greece and the EFSF, on the ESM and the OMT[1] resolution of the European Central Bank have—*de facto* and unintentionally—compensated for deficits in the political and parliamentary process, and thereby contributed not inconsiderably to the acceptance of the decisions in question.

II. EROSION OF THE LEGACY

The authority of the law has suffered. Under the conditions of globalization, European integration, and the overlapping of state powers, the core of the state under the rule of law, namely the containment of politics by law (Kant), has become ineffective. From "forget about the Treaty" in the context of the Euro crisis, via central political guidelines at state level, to the underhand implementation of state law through the administration of the *Länder* (for example, nuclear law, immigration and asylum law, compulsory military service)—the cases when politics has disregarded the law or does not take containment by the law seriously have increased over recent years. Even in jurisdiction there are calls for a relaxation of the rule of law in the interest of more fairness in individual cases, which is even being implemented through marginal legal interpretations in isolated instances.

1. Although the European Union is a community based on the rule of law and integration has been undertaken by means of the law itself over the last 60 years, dealings with the law are sometimes surprisingly "generous." This begins with the way in which regulations concerning changes to Treaties are dealt with (e.g. the belated implementation of Article 136 [3] TFEU). It continues with the management of the distribution of competences (e.g. the patent portfolio) and the procedure for making decisions within EU institutions (e.g. in the legislative procedure on conflicting trilogues laid down in the Treaty, or the secondary legislation amendment to required

majorities as prescribed in primary law), and ends with the current refugee and financial crisis. For example, the history of the European currency union is also a story in which the relevant regulations have been put aside again and again to comply with the interests of the moment. This was the case from the start, when Italy and Belgium were admitted as Members at the beginning in spite of a total debt that was 100% above permitted limits, and continues today where sanctions stipulated in the Treaty are not implemented or set at zero despite long-term breach of the Treaty's debt guidelines (the so-called Maastricht criteria). Of course one must wonder whether it is sensible to impose additional financial sanctions on Member States who are in financial difficulties, and there is something to be said in favor of changing this. But if such regulations are established, they may not be disowned, as otherwise citizens' trust in the integrity of institutions is damaged. Selective obedience to the law cannot continue over the long term.

2. Excessive complexity of laws is not based on a fundamentally hostile attitude of political actors towards the law, but the consequences are the same. The ever-more complicated reality of everyday life makes the political management of state and society more difficult, and

so it resorts to an increasingly open and definitive codification of modern laws. Of course the effect of this in practice is also increasingly difficult to predict. Added to this is the commitment to Community legislation with its sclerotic tendencies, the so-called *acquis communautaire* of EU law. In substance this consists of around 150,000 legal instruments in secondary and tertiary European law, which can only be altered at the initiative of the European Commission with a qualified majority of Member States and with the assent of the European Parliament—that is, in practice, with great difficulty—and which have an impact on all aspects of life. This makes coherent political management difficult even at EU level, but especially so at the level of Member States and increases the inclination not to take containment by the law seriously. Examples in all Member States are legion, and range from data retention via mail-order pharmacies to road tolls.

In Germany the authority of the law is additionally undermined by the ill-considered way of dealing with the state system, focusing on day-to-day political needs. The specific structure of federalism makes the law more and more complicated and prone to error when it comes to administration and justice. Constitution-altering legislation has subjected this structure to fundamental reforms in 1994, 2006, and

2009, and another reorganization is scheduled for 2017. But this lacks an overarching concept: while the *Länder* were to be protected from the threat of the unitary federal state in 1994, the aim of the first reform of the federal system, undertaken in 2006, was to disentangle the competences of federal and *Land* governments to make decision-making easier and responsibilities identifiable. In 2009, after three years, a complete about-face took place with the second reform of the federal system, and the imbrication of the two levels was re-intensified. This process is still going on, as the 2010 safeguarding of joint offices (ARGEs) and *Optionskommunen* (optional local management) in Article 91(e) GG shows, which is now expected to result in a veritable surge of centralization comprising opaque domains of state and *Land* government. This will hardly be conducive to the authority of the law.

3. In addition to this we can see the increasing social marginalization of lawyers. A so-called monopoly of lawyers has existed in Germany's public administration since the 19th century, and lawyers were well represented on the boards of large companies too. They have gradually lost these positions—not least because of a lack of interdisciplinary compatibility and their own structural skepticism—because they were perceived as

expressing doubts in the face of innovation and to this extent seen as conservative. For the post-1968 dominant mainstream this is unattractive, and economists, who could always offer suitable explanations, were the more attractive partner even for liberals; for a time, their discipline was even given the role of an "imperial science." These observations may be dismissed as the professionally motivated carping of losers, but the increasing marginalization of lawyers from key positions in society also has detrimental consequences for the importance and authority of the law.

In the period after 1949, a consensus had emerged that the unconditional protection of the law was part of our society's identity not just in terms of constitutional law, and that this was a civilizing achievement; but since 1990 this seems to be steadily changing. Today the constitutional requirements of jurisdiction and procedure in decision-making may seem a legal trifle to some, but this loses sight of the fact that it is precisely these requirements that are the guarantors of legitimacy and legal security. This might also have something to do with the fact that—in society as a whole—lawyers are in retreat. Bärbel Bohley's famous statement, "We wanted justice and got the rule of law," can be understood not just as a laconic reference to the fact that injustices and hardships exist even in the state under the rule of law. It can also be seen as a subversive justification for flouting the law in the interests of individual ideas of justice or morality. This was precisely the argument made by senior church leaders during the refugee crisis of 2015/16, for example, not with regard to their own actions, which they considered legitimate, but with regard to state officials. So-called "church asylum" is another illustration of the fact that increasingly the law has to take a stand against (individual) morality.

III. CONSEQUENCES

The containment of politics by law is an indispensable condition of a state and social system that are based on freedom, equality, and self-determination, and is an achievement of civilization. To secure this for the future as well requires, in light of what we have just discussed: 1. A substantial reduction in the quantity of regulations at all levels; 2–4. A clear distribution of competences between the levels and mechanisms that encourage political actors to assume responsibility; and 5. The abandonment of particular moral attitudes.

PETER M. HUBER

1. Fewer laws also mean fewer risks for disobeying the law and a greater chance of implementing applicable law and its authority. For this reason, all regulations in secondary and tertiary law of the European Union should be provided with so-called "sunset clauses" to prevent them becoming sclerotic and to make way for new decisions that are appropriate to the problems. At state level better coordination between the responsibilities of legislating and implementation is required to reduce the overburdening of administration and justice and to prevent the gulf between "is" and "ought" from becoming even wider.

2. The citizen must be able to see who is responsible for what, and that responsibilities are exercised effectively. In multi-level systems of EU, state government, and *Länder* a functioning division of competences oriented towards the spirit of subsidiarity is thus required. The same is applicable, *mutatis mutandis*, in the relationship between state government and *Land*. Situations where administration or finance overlap are to be avoided as far as possible.

3. Sound legislation, the integration of legislation into the system, and a certain amount of slowness are more important than effectiveness and speed. Trilogues

should thus be avoided in the European Parliament and the legislative procedure set down in Treaties carried out. At the same time, the role of national parliaments in the legislative procedure of the Union should be strengthened. Above all they need more time. For example, members of the German Bundestag must frequently vote on wide-ranging national treaties or submissions under European law, although they do not have a German text and are under considerable time pressure. How can they know exactly what they are voting on, how to make the necessary compromises, and how to evaluate the consequences for individual sectors of society?

4. It is, however, the task of politics to reduce the existing complexity of decision-making structures wherever possible, and not evade its responsibility in connection with these decision-making structures, or even take advantage of them. The solution of complex problems also requires a clear allocation of responsibility—at all state levels. Referenda and plebiscites can be helpful, as here the question of responsibility cannot be avoided.

5. In the free state under the rule of law there is no binding morality. In light of this, appealing to

individual notions of morality and justice or political considerations of expediency cannot justify deviation from the law. The state under the rule of law exists through the law or it does not exist.

Note

1. EFSF = European Financial Stability Facility; ESM = European Stability Mechanism; OMT = Outright Monetary Transactions.

CHAPTER 8

WHO ADMINISTRATES THE
RULE OF LAW?

WOLFGANG SCHÖN

The law lives through its authority. This authority is
not restricted to the law being obeyed by the citizen.
Before it can be respected and obeyed by the citizen,
the law must also be understood, explained, and its
meaning recognized in each individual case. In public
authorities and companies, in law courts and lawyers'
chambers, in academic departments and training
colleges, there must be enough people who know
how the law works. Merely publishing a regulation
in Germany's *Federal Law Gazette* does not influence
people's behavior as if by magic. And the content of

the law is often not clear without outside help, even to those with the best will in the world. Compliance with the law depends on legal certainty. Legal certainty depends on legal clarity. And legal clarity depends on smart brains whose judgment can be relied upon.

Thus there can be no rule of law without "capacities" to administrate the rule of law. In economic and political debates this mantra has long been applied to developing and emerging nations. For some years "capacity building" has been one of the most vital tasks for international organizations seeking to help volatile states find internal stability. Today the education of judges, the training of tax officials, the schooling of police forces, but also their appropriate financial and material equipment are part of the standard program for the development of many African, Asian, and Latin American communities. For a long time the West has fancied that its capacities were sufficiently large to manage its own legal production in a suitable way. But is that really the case? Are we still in a position to run our state under the rule of law? Do even European states, and Germany in particular, need a shot of "capacity building" in order to increase their competence and effectiveness, but also their legal security and decision-making power?

The demands placed on our state under the rule of law have risen steadily over the last few decades. And the rate of change of these demands has gone up just as steadily. This trend towards the creation of legal provisions restricts both the public authorities and the citizens. In the case of government entities, constitutional and administrative litigation has, over decades, developed an almost seamless system of "judicial review" for decisions taken by authorities, a system that drastically reduces material judgment as well as substantive creativity, and that has at the same time opened up a time-consuming avenue of legal appeal. In the case of private undertakings, the continual expansion of civil and criminal liability has led to the situation that today personal—particularly commercial—decisions carry considerable legal risks alongside the obvious economic risks. The confrontation with the criminal law in particular has an almost paralyzing effect: a shareholder's complaint will seem unpleasant and troublesome to any board member of a large company, but the investigations of a public prosecutor will appear extremely serious and a threat to the company's livelihood.

This essay does not aim to complain vociferously about the ongoing trend to submit the state, the social and the economic life to ever narrower legal

WOLFGANG SCHÖN

requirements. That has happened often enough. This development is probably unavoidable and correlates with the growing technical, economic, and social complexity of our lives. Rather, the question is whether we possess the capacities to support this process of creating legal provisions in an appropriate way, that is, whether we possess the financial, personal, and intellectual resources to give the diverse legal environments a measure of security and clarity that facilitates the legitimate activities of the state and of private undertakings (within a reasonable time-frame).

In so doing we encounter a central problem that I should like to call the "problem of elites"—a problem that has a dual aspect: personal/intellectual on the one hand, financial on the other.

We first encounter the "problem of elites" in the production of legal standards. Legislation originates from specialist units within ministries, both in state government and in the *Länder*. It is reviewed in parliamentary procedure by expert representatives of associations and academic scholars, and when it passes into practice it is commented on and monitored by a few leading practitioners. These groups of people possess the educational background, the time, and the intellect to understand, discuss, and polish even highly complex bodies of regulation. The legal product that is created in this way affects a large number of citizens (but also civil servants, legal advisors, and in-house lawyers) who do not have comparable capacities, who are pressed for time and are often substantively overstretched, but who are nevertheless tasked with making this law a reality. What is a playground for experts appears to the normal user as by turns a labyrinth, a rollercoaster, and hall of mirrors. While the mass of legal material and the amount of changes involved can barely be managed quantitatively, many qualitative demands are added that overstretch not just the interested layperson.

To act correctly in this context requires quite considerable legal capacities in every respect. And this is where the financial "problem of elites" comes in. Only a few actors—large companies in particular—have the financial resources, but also the necessary economies of scale to master the profusion of legal material and legal risks even remotely well. Many other players—small and medium-sized enterprises especially—are not in a position to do this, although the quantity and nature of the legal norms applicable to them are not markedly fewer. They can neither set up large legal departments nor to a large extent purchase the services of expensive legal chambers. By contrast, large companies can use their economies of scale to give themselves a competitive edge even in the management of legal risks. In public administration it is not necessarily any different: a growing need for qualified personnel is confronted with constant cost pressures from government and an increasingly uncompetitive civil service salary structure. Large-scale projects—such as the management of floods of refugees—require highly motivated and well-trained staff who can deliver legally required justice in each individual case and effectively cope with mass operations at the same time. The real capacities do not necessarily correspond to this. What are the consequences?

When high-level legal demands come up against low-level legal capacities, these capacities must react to the obvious deficit. In my opinion we can identify two typical kinds of reaction:

One reaction is to behave in a risk-averse way. Wanting to avoid mistakes and penalties means striving to remain always "on the safe side." This reduces risks but also decreases opportunities at the same time, as legal insecurity and lack of information and capacity lead, in the case of risk-averse actors, to legal margins for maneuver being left unexplored, as a considerable (objectively too large) safe distance from the boundaries of the permissible is maintained. Alternatively, one engages in hedging strategies (aided by voluminous documentation and legal opinions) which, again, only a few players can access financially.

Another—risky—kind of behavior can be seen in the case of people who "chance it" and act despite unresolved legal risks. They regard legal uncertainty as an existential risk that one does not want to enter into lightly, but that one must enter into under actual (or economic) pressure, not least because the competitors (often the foreign competitors) are not experiencing comparable difficulties or are ignoring them too. If a public administration acts in such a way, there is a danger of despotism and oppression. If the citizen or a company acts in such a way, the rule of law becomes a game of roulette for them. The private individual as a gambler in the legal casino—that should not become a long-term perspective.

The overall situation becomes particularly problematic when capacity problems affect several concerned parties. Let us look at the case of managers who behave in a potentially criminal way: if there were a reliable common understanding of the criminal limits of business activities both in companies' legal departments and with the prosecuting authorities, all would be well served, that is, compliance and legal security would be created, enabling sensible business activity. In reality, however, in the case of complex factual and legal investigations, public prosecutors also want to be "on the safe side," and so do not want to waive a penalty claim independently. The consequence is that the prosecuting authorities often make excessive demands in some instances, and press charges in case of doubt. This is counterbalanced in the companies by management boards and legal departments whose tendency to be risk averse is further increased by this behavior. The internal cost of compliance is driven upwards, with the result that finally, through mutual escalation, a maximum is developed as the "standard" for correct behavior, far exceeding the desired optimum. The representatives of the state and of the citizens paralyze each other in a state of collective legal uncertainty.

What is to be done? An impartial observer might see three options:

• An expansion of legal capacities, enlarging public administrations, expanding legal departments, and improving wage structures. This would reduce risks, enable swift agreements between the interested parties, and even improve the common understanding of what is right and wrong. But the rule of law does not come free. And everyone knows that a purely quantitative extension of legal capacities does not necessarily entail its intellectual enhancement. There comes a point when the surplus value of a simply quantitative expansion of legal expertise no longer justifies the costs involved.

• A dismantling of legal requirements. This is easier said than done. The effort that has been put into limiting the flood of legal standards over the past few decades is enormous and has still brought forth few results. On closer examination there are only a few legal provisions that are not justified. And the central problem of legal uncertainty does not correlate with the amount of legal material: in a complex economic and legal world, a reduction in written law can even lead to an increase in legal risks, if one creates new loopholes and one is not prepared to extend dramatically the scope of freedom of public administration and of the citizen in their respective areas of competence.

• A reduction of the risks associated with legal uncertainty. As we have shown, the central problem in the decision-making behavior of actors in both state and society/economy lies in the fact that legal uncertainty can be linked to high risks in the form of draconian penalties. Criminal law stands at the pinnacle of this movement, but other disadvantages in terms of legal liability or administrative sanctions can also have enormous effects. This must be re-thought. Action from a position of uncertainty should not as such be regarded with suspicion. Corrections can be imposed, but not always necessarily with hard, retrospective penalties. The citizen must be aware that the administration will not always share his legal viewpoint, and that his demands can be rejected. But this refusal must not necessarily be linked to drastic reputational damage or liability regulations that seriously jeopardize the citizens' bona fide activities.

For this reason, the authorities applying the rule of law must not give up on enforcement. They may make stringent demands—on public administration, on citizens, and on companies. But it may not offload the risk of legal uncertainty on those whom it requires to act in uncertainty (often at short notice). The resolution of legal uncertainty may only be covered by costs that the state and citizens can bear without their ability to act being fundamentally curtailed and their productive freedom being restricted beyond what is necessary. The authority of the law thus also depends on clarity with regard to its boundaries—the boundaries between right and wrong.

CHAPTER 9

POWER FRAGMENTATION, VIOLENCE AND THE AUTHORITY OF LAW – A LOOK AT CONTEMPORARY ARMED CONFLICTS

PETER MAURER

AUTHORITY AND AUTHORITIES

Broadly speaking, authority refers to personal, institutional, or social positioning, to hierarchy within the state, private enterprise, religious structures, professional life, civil society, and more; you can take a formal or *de facto* perspective, envisage authority based on force, power, consent, acquiescence, physical, intellectual, or moral factors and any combination of them. You may dwell on characteristics of its flipside concept—"legitimacy"—and reference Max Weber's traditional, charismatic, and institutional legitimacy. There is an abundance of perspectives under which one can consider the transformation of authority.

HUMANITARIAN PERSPECTIVE

I am speaking to you today from the perspective of a humanitarian institution, which has worked for more than 150 years on the frontlines of war and violence to preserve humanity through law, to influence policy-making and to assist and protect people.

This work is connected in many ways to authority and authorities: there are legal connections, because we have been given a mandate and thus a kind of delegated authority by states through the Geneva Conventions (the largest ratified legal instrument worldwide), to support states in the implementation and development of international humanitarian law; policy connections, because of our role to engage with states and non-state parties in a neutral, impartial, and independent way, so that they have adequate human-itarian policies in place; and operational connectors, through our work supplementing, supporting, and substituting authorities through humanitarian action.

This perspective offers some insight on which I will elaborate with regard to various aspects: possible failures of authorities to respond to people's aspirations; the transformation of authority on the battlefield; the impact of such transformation on the authority of the law; the cost for individuals and communities when authority breaks down; and the possibility of reconstituting authority through neutral and impartial humanitarian action.

FAILURES OF AND TRANSFORMATION OF AUTHORITY

If you want to measure what happened to authority in and around armed conflict over the last 150 years, let us first take a look at how the International Committee of the Red Cross (ICRC) evolved as an institution. From five founding fathers and some volunteers, it has become an organization of 15,000 professional staff worldwide, with operations in more than 80 countries and an annual budget of SFr.1.6 billion. The ICRC can also be found at the core of the Red Cross and Red Crescent movements, with more than 100 million members and 17 million active volunteers engaged in humanitarian work worldwide. It has grown at the same pace at which authorities in states and societies failed to assist and protect their own people. Its engagement started with the "wounded and sick in the field," focused on prisoners of war and detainees more generally during World War I, and shifted attention increasingly onto civilians in the aftermath of World War II. Alongside its work promoting respect for the law in state armies, the Red Cross focused attention over decades on an increasing number of non-state armed groups. It also engaged prominently on the prohibition or limitation of the use of weapons. And it has become an authority in its own right, struggling to encourage, support, and facilitate respect for humanitarian laws and principles and to help ensure compliance with those norms.

For an organization such as the ICRC the transformation of authority is therefore not merely an abstract question, but has been a daily experience throughout our history. This is all the more true today since, over the past couple of years, failure of policy dialogue and diplomacy has in many places taken armed conflict to a new level of radicalism and impact on people. This has left us with a paradoxical situation: while we live in an increasingly globalized civilization, with more people than ever in the history of humankind connected, educated, healthy, and wealthy, and with institutions and authorities constantly improving their performance, we simultaneously see a lack of access to basic services, high levels of violence, economic injustice, poor governance, and corruption in an increasingly wide area of the world. More than 700 million people are living below poverty lines and well over two billion people live in fragile states and experience conditions of fragility in more countries than ever.

QUESTIONING EXISTING AUTHORITIES

It is the very essence of conflict that authority is questioned and challenged. Violence is often the direct consequence of the antagonisms of power between multiple actors and authorities or the result of the exclusion from power. Take the so-called Arab Spring and the violence that ensued: the beginning was a rebellion, not of the poor against the rich, not of terrorists against legitimate state power, but of people experiencing injustice, discrimination, and marginalization by their respective authorities and exclusion from authority in the state.

In many places where we operate, we see conflicting relationships between different religious, political, tribal, economic, and social dividing lines, with a high prevalence of violence and little or no legitimate political processes leading to consensus about the society's future. We see a lack of engagement to prevent violence, or to stop armed conflicts. We encounter strong beliefs on all sides of the frontlines that violence will, in the end, offer better options than the present situation or a political process, which is experienced by too many as one of discrimination, exclusion, injustice, poverty—or in short, failed integration. In many societies, we see no appetite for living together with those members of the community who are on the other side of the dividing line, and therefore no wish to organize institutions and the community together. Many of the regions in which we operate simply lack authorities that take account of social diversity. These are situations in which, as humanitarians, we have to say that we need political solutions. We cannot fix these problems through humanitarianism. Only a legitimate and inclusive political process among the key stakeholders can, at the end of the day, lead societies out of armed conflict and build inclusive societies. Pending such processes humanitarian actors may have a distinctive role to play and something to offer.

FRAGMENTED POWERS IN TODAY'S
BATTLEFIELDS

The overwhelming feature of today's conflicts, in which ICRC is working, is the fragmentation of powers and authorities; de-structured conflicts with unclear command, control, and communication; continuously changing alliances; as well as long-term and high levels of violence with a deep social impact. We are talking about the Middle East (Syria, Iraq, Yemen, Israel/Palestine, or Libya), about the Lake Chad Region, the Horn of Africa, or the two Sudans, about Afghanistan—and, yes, about Europe (Ukraine, Nagorno-Karabakh), and many more.

In these contexts, a number of state and non-state actors—in conflict regions and beyond—are clashing in an increasing number of battlefields. Moreover, states are operating with armed forces in secret or remote mode, using drones, robotics, and other sophisticated cyber-technologies, while non-state actors, pretending and aspiring to be states, are taking over state-like functions, such as water supplies, hospitals, schools, and local police forces. From Hamas to Hezbollah, from Al-Nusra to Islamic State, from the Taliban to Boko Haram, it is rare that any of these groups exists in an exclusively military dimension. They aspire to be—and are—authorities for the populations under their control and to whom they deliver social services.

AUTHORITARIAN EXERCISE OF POWER

While the dominant feature of authority in the battle-field is fragmentation, we often witness the opposite within conflicting parties. The paradox is that while authority is fragmented and fragmenting in many places, authoritarian power is expanding within the different groups. This again makes conflicts even more "violence prone," as Amartya Sen has described it so well in his remarkable work *Iↄentity anↄ Violence.*

LACK OF COMPLIANCE AND TRUST IN THE LAW

With fragmentation and violence comes—most visibly for us—the evaporation of trust into the law of war, which has a deep impact on the authority of the legal framework. Most elementary rules of behavior are violated in many of today's conflicts. And while this is nothing new as such—we have after all seen world wars and genocides and crimes against humanity for 150 years—some of today's dynamics may be particular.

These dynamics are actually quite simple. Normally belligerents know that military force should exercise caution and that civilians have to be protected, women and children spared, hospitals not attacked, detainees treated humanely and not tortured. But in many places where we interact with them, we see that they lack the confidence that the other side will implement the law as well. It is this lack of trust in reciprocity that leads to the dynamic of disrespect. The laws of war as a moral and practical authority, rooted in customs and in the consent of belligerents over centuries, lack authority under such circumstances. The totalitarian rhetoric and practice of today's warfare, the de-humanization of the adversary, hyper-politicization of the law, which is used primarily to publically expose the adversary, the stigmatization of the adversary, double standards in the application of the law—all these factors contribute to the perception of laws that are systematically disrespected. For decades international humanitarian law (IHL) has been the under-the-radar discipline of the militaries, their lawyers, academics, and the ICRC, trying to find practical solutions for the impasse between military necessity and the protection of civilians in the midst of conflict. Today, violations of

IHL unfold in a highly communicative environment, which is becoming a kind of extended battlefield with one side accusing the other and vice versa of violations of the Geneva Conventions, war crimes and crimes against humanity; and all sides using legal account-ability as a political tool rather than an obvious and non-political consequence of violations of the law. As the law becomes a political propaganda tool, the trust of belligerents that the law is here to serve them and their roles in combat is rapidly being eroded.

While the dominant story in the news talks about indiscriminate terrorist attacks in an increasing number of cities worldwide, in reality this only reflects the evaporation of any regulatory authority. It is more obvious by the day that we lack consensus about a shared humanity and about minimal stand-ards of behavior in many of today's conflicts. In many places, therefore, we see hardly any difference in the behavior of state and non-state actors. Our empirical data on attacks on healthcare services in eleven coun-tries shows that state and non-state armed groups are almost equally responsible for such violations. It also shows that in conflict settings both state forces and non-state armed groups are much more likely to attack healthcare services—hospitals, ambulances, doctors, and patients—than organized criminal groups or individuals. Those with weapons aspire to provide services, but they also aspire to the authority to deny services to their enemies, real or perceived.

When minimal common ground is lacking between belligerents, when there is no common humanity as the basis of authority, wars have no limits and therefore no end. You all know the evolution too well. While the majority of victims in World War I were soldiers, during World War II, much more totalitarian than the first, we saw more civilian than military victims. Today's civilian casualties are hardly "collateral damage"; civilians are the primary targets of belligerents in warfare and this reflects a stark lack of confidence in and respect for the law.

Paradoxically again, civilians are also the objects of competition between states and non-state actors who are struggling to display their ability to provide public order and social services and thus stabilize their authority over people and territory. Not least because of this trend, humanitarian action is increasingly politicized. In many conflict regions, therefore, combining the use of force with a politicized delivery of humanitarian services to people in order to garner their support is a popular formula. Russian convoys to Eastern Ukraine undoubtedly meet people's crucial needs, but they come with a political twist as much as the deliberately erratic provision/denial of access to neutral humanitarian actors in Syria and many other places.

My point here is that further escalation of violence and combats will not stop the negative spiral of violence and violations of norms and the difficulty of delivering neutral, impartial, and independent humanitarian services: there is no victory through military force and violence around the corner. If anything, rebuilding consensus on the validity and importance of the law and the principles of humanitarian action will be crucial. This is why ICRC considers our front-line engagement and negotiations with parties to conflicts with the objective of respecting the norms and opening humanitarian spaces the most important humanitarian contribution to rebuilding authority in society. But I will come back to this at the end.

Let me add one more challenge with regard to laws and norms, which is connected to the technological evolution of warfare. International humanitarian laws and principles were drafted at a time when war was strongly connected to kinetic power, clearly delineated battlefields, and structured, organized armed actors. Today's technological developments, cyber-warfare, remote warfare capacity, and robotics in particular, are potentially globalizing battlefields, questioning the lines between civilian and military actors and blurring responsibility between human commanders and artificial intelligence. While these developments affect many areas of life, they are certainly difficult to handle as we try to adjust and adapt traditional norms to these new realities.

IMPACT OF TRANSFORMING AUTHORITIES ON PEOPLE

When authorities fail, power fragments and violence is triggered, the effects on people, economies, societies, and political dynamics are massive and often go beyond a national and regional impact.

What we encounter in today's conflicts is no longer just a temporary, localized disruption of lives and livelihoods. The impact of the breakdown of functioning authorities is myriad: it can be systemic (affecting water, health, education systems); long-term (see presence of ICRC in key conflicts); contagious (it moves from political into criminal, inter-community violence and into criminal economic structures); it has both a direct (people wounded and killed) and an indirect impact on people; it is felt regionally and globally (the record numbers of forcibly displaced people demonstrate this); it is primarily happening in strongly urbanized contexts, where vulnerabilities are greatest and the cumulative impact of violence most clearly felt (this is particularly disturbing as two-thirds of global GDP is generated by 600 cities, and the proportion is rising). The estimated overall cost of this vicious circle has reached the staggering figure of US$12–14 trillion per year or more than ten percent of global GDP. International humanitarian assistance almost doubled in the last ten years and surpassed the United Nations' peace-keeping operations budget, totaling more than US$25 billion. Record numbers of people displaced by violence are fleeing within and beyond their countries (two-thirds of the displaced are displaced within their own countries and are therefore technically not refugees). Displacement and violence goes far beyond warfare. Out of the 50 most violent cities, 47 are in Latin America (in Brazil alone, last year, as many people died from firearms as there were war victims in Syria, illustrating that other forms of violence, which are not strictly speaking armed conflict have a massive impact on people and societies).

Given these staggering numbers, we are now confronted with an important gap between the needs of people suffering from violence and the breakdown of authority and authorities delivering social services on the one hand, and the ability of humanitarian actors to respond to those needs on the other hand.

WHAT CAN BE DONE?

Of course, the standard programs of humanitarian actors make sense: scale-up operations, enlarge the donor base, cooperate more broadly with local institutions and with the private sector, build partnerships for greater impact, innovate and make humanitarian action more efficient and effective.

But all these efforts—as important as they may be—are hardly the most relevant contribution in light of the challenges we are facing.

When authority and authorities are questioned, fragmented, and the spiral of violence is unrelenting, what is most lacking is the ability to rebuild trust, to build consensus among all parties around neutral, impartial, and independent humanitarian action and to negotiate a humanitarian space, which reflects a minimum of communality among belligerents. This may help, in a very modest way and through humanitarian work, to promote the idea of a rule-based society and to recreate some trust among parties to conflict. The ICRC undertakes simple things such as exchanging Red Cross messages and allegations of arrest across frontlines; trying to access detainees to ensure humane treatment and give at least some signs of life to families about the whereabouts of their detained relatives; making deliberate efforts to bring families together, who have been displaced throughout regions and beyond; delivering, whenever possible, humanitarian assistance across frontlines to service needs on all sides of the conflict; negotiating security arrangements with all parties to ensure success for our operations and safety for our staff.

Engaging with all parties across frontlines is important to give concrete meaning to international humanitarian law. Access to besieged areas needs to be negotiated; humanitarian convoys need the security guarantees of all sides in a conflict. When violations of international humanitarian law happen, our delegates engage with parties to the conflict in order to change their behavior and to better protect civilians. We sensitize parties about the importance of rules, knowing that these rules must be continuously interpreted in the field to give them concrete meaning. We create space for dialogue and compromise and we support people in some of the most difficult situations in their own efforts to protect themselves and to step into the gaps of non-existent and weak authorities.

All these approaches are terribly modest in ambition and result. Yet preserving a minimal space for humanity is in our experience—and in the majority of the most difficult situations—the first and most critical step in rebuilding authority, reconnecting communities with political leaders, and injecting hope where hope has been lost.

Such an approach seems to be in stark contradiction to the political mood of our time, when the fight against extremism and terrorism is the dominating trend and the public rhetoric of war occupies everyone's attention. This is a misunderstanding. As a humanitarian organization, the Red Cross does not take sides in *jus a* *bellum* issues or with regard to the legitimacy of the use of force to fight terrorism. However, we do strongly recommend a cautious approach in the use of force and the recognition that, when force is used, a common space of humanity must be preserved.

This approach also seems at odds with the impression that today's extremists are not really willing to enter into a conversation such as the one described above. But we should not draw hasty conclusions. Too often have we seen rhetorical and conceptual exclusion become real exclusion, only to understand, ten years later, that a consistent attempt to keep doors open for dialogue was necessary. Indeed, our experience is that humanitarian action can keep the space for dialogue open so that a minimum of humanity can be preserved and authority recreated. This is by no means easy, but the alternative is certainly worse.

CHAPTER 10

BIG DATA AND THE DIGITAL REVOLUTION IN LAW

THOMAS HOEREN

The digital transformation is in full swing. The changes affect not only the areas of "digital" law such as information law, IT law, data protection, or telecommunications law, but the law as a whole. For example, in the case of the German Civil Code [BGB] traditional civil law too is being put to the test. In the background there lurks the question of what demands big data will make of constitutional law.

THOMAS HOEREN

BIG DATA AND CONSTITUTIONAL LAW

The points of intersection between big data and constitutional law are less specific than conceptual. For example, changes in the importance of the protection of fundamental rights are up for discussion. The practical importance of the protection of the traditional rights of the individual is disappearing in the relationship between state and citizen. Until now civil liberties were considered laws protecting the citizen from the state. In a digital society, however, the protection of the citizen against all-powerful Internet companies such as Facebook or Google has become more important. In national constitutional law this increases the requirement of concretizing the official form of the objective, legal dimension and of emphasizing the duty of the state to offer protection against the frenzy of data collection perpetrated by those in Silicon Valley, for example. The same applies to EU and national law. Consideration of transnational, primarily European, multi-level associations is essential.

BIG DATA GOVERNANCE

In the age of big data the regulation of data-assisted processes is facing new challenges. For a long time now considerably more actors than state, economy, and users have been involved. Following the question of "code is law" (Lawrence Lessig), both those who are involved technically—above all programmers—and the algorithms themselves are being given increasing importance. Promising, but by no means exhaustive approaches to the sustainable regulation of big data are reflected in concepts such as data protection through technology in particular. Although data protec-tion in the guise of the new European General Data Protection Regulation has just been adopted, in the era of self-learning algorithms, autonomous systems, and the Internet of Things (IoT) its primacy is increasingly in doubt. What answers and regulatory options can the law draw on in such cases (e.g. the rise in telecom-munications law in the case of self-driving cars)?

DATA OWNERSHIP

On the question of whether claims to sole rights exist with regard to data, the legal system provides at best limited insights. With regard to ownership, which addresses the question of corporeal objects (Sections 90, 902 BGB), the issue of data having an independent, physically tangible existence can be ruled out. Even an analogous application of this provision of property law raises the problem of the extent to which principles such as the public availability and traceability of data are guaranteed. In particular it is questionable whether data—understood as the basis of information—allow exclusive assignment. Arguing in favor of this are, for example, Sections 398, 413, and 453 BGB that allow the assignment and transfer of legal positions. Attempts to construct an exclusive assignment of data laws via provisions regarding the transfer of ownership through processing (Section 950 BGB) lead only to lukewarm results. Ultimately, in the context of these claims it would have to be clarified once again which legal positions are being infringed upon. In any event, points of intersection with criminal law and the latter's provisions for the protection of information and economic interests can provide indications for the assignment of data and their usage, as, for example, the act of writing the data on a data carrier in the bills of exchange law provides information about the beneficiaries. Apart from that, reference can be made to the informational concern which is illustrated in law in the data protection law regarding personal data or legitimate interests of confidentiality (Section 17, Act Against Unfair Competition [UWG]), for example. This considers the exclusivity rights that are involved in aiming to restrict the information commodity to the benefit of the person in possession of the confidential information. How this fits in with the copyrighted collection of data as a database (system) remains to be seen.

DATA AS PAYMENT

Compounding the abovementioned problem is the categorization of data as a paid service. As an economic factor in and compensation for otherwise unpaid (Internet) services, the provision and task of data sovereignty is a characteristic of the digital revolution. This might become relevant through new kinds of contracts and by being taken into account by secondary law, for example through the reversal of relationships covered by the law of obligations. In particular, participation and licensing models for the use of data as information might make sense. In the case of underage young people, it is problematic whether the providing of data to social networks or the like is not legally disadvantageous, and thus the majority of the contracts covered by this are ineffective.

DATA QUALITY

An essential factor in the valorization of data is their quality. By this we mean two aspects: on the one hand technical legibility and processability, and on the other the accuracy of the information represented by the data. This has a role to play for example in the purchase of data files and contractual guarantees. Among other things, it must be decided whether and how the average type and quality of data can be determined, that is which IT standards serve as a basis for the technical processing of data.

DATA IN INSOLVENCY CASES

Increasingly, private individuals, authorities, and companies store services and data files in the Cloud. Up to now this has worked smoothly, but in the medium term a question arises: what happens to a customer's data files in the case of the provider's insolvency? Unlike the case of classic commodities, data lack the corporeality inherent in the concept of ownership (see above). The separation of data in the case of insolvency according to Section 47 of Germany's Insolvency Statute [InsO] brings its own particular challenges, especially with regard to its identifiability. Currently the "data owner" will base his right to recover possession on positions established under the law of obligations. A quasi right *in rem* applied to an individual piece of data itself could provide more legal certainty. Equally, other approaches to making insolvency law sound with regard to digitization are conceivable. For example, Luxembourg has recently created a dedicated right to recover possession with regard to data in cases of insolvency that sets up clear criteria for implementation (Art. 567, para. 2 Code de Commerce).

BIG DATA AND PRIVACY

The efficient regulation in accordance with data protection law of big data analytics and other big data applications represents another important task for the law. Concepts such as "privacy by design" and "privacy by default" can create a successful framework, and the requirement for this is a high degree of transparency with regard to the assumed criteria and precepts.

Auditing, monitoring, and independent certification offer additional starting points. Expiry and deletion dates must be clearly specified, and opportunities for de-anonymizing the data must be prevented. The conditions and scope of the instruments of consent used in the valorization of context-related data must be clearly defined.

SMART CONTRACTS

The use of smart contracts is gaining in importance. By this we mean automated protocols that ensure the execution of a contract (in real time) according to tailor-made algorithms. In the best-case scenario, this results in the interests of the contractual parties being adequately represented without requiring a mediation agency to help either party to implement the terms of the contract. Nevertheless, the protocol for creating synallagmatic—that is reciprocal—parity would have to take account of the interests of all parties in a transparent and balanced way. This might necessitate a requirement for regulation that takes account of the rights and duties involved in automated business transactions.

M2M: MACHINE-TO-MACHINE COMMUNICATION AND IT SECURITY

The automation of contracts has an impact on industry and the Internet of Things most of all. If we give machines responsibility to carry out "autonomous" decisions and interactions with other devices, IT security must be guaranteed against outside interference. We could add to this orders and tasks whose handling, in the absence of a direct, human declaration of intent, becomes suspect. The automatic ordering of replacement parts and raw materials by industrial machines and the subsequent automated implementation by the receiver unit render human interactions obsolete and in turn require a legal framework.

CIVIL LIABILITY 4.0

The introduction of new technologies such as big data forecasts, self-driving cars, or intelligent industrial robots presents a challenge to the liability laws of the German Civil Code (BGB). Who is liable if damages are caused as a result of incorrect decisions taken by autonomous systems and self-learning algorithms? In such cases the principle of fault-based liability is stretched to the limit. Thus in the case of self-driving cars the system of vehicle holder liability without fault as per Section 7 of the German Road Traffic Act [StVG] is often used. Outside road traffic laws, however, there are no comparable absolute offences. So should a specific absolute liability be created for autonomous systems—for example following the example of Section 833 BGB (Liability of Animal Keeper)? Or can the problem be solved by the established regimes of liability?

BIG DATA AND COMPETITION LAW

In both the digital and non-digital markets, numerous companies generate high turnovers using business models that are based on the collection and processing of data. In competition law, interesting aspects arise against this backdrop with regard to so-called "data advantage" and questions of data sparseness. Data advantage can be seen above all in the opportunity major players have for "cross-usage," whereby they can produce data files that cannot be replicated by competitors. And although data is actually a non-competing commodity, in practice it is often only obtainable at such high costs that it is *de facto* exclusive. This is where competition law is needed.

AND WHAT'S NEXT?

No one knows what the future holds—politicians of many nations are currently speculating how we can organize the digital transformation in a way that is efficient and fair in legal terms. Potentially we need new forms of legislation, for example using laws with fixed "sell-by dates", moratoria that include phases of conscious non-regulation, codes of conduct, and a universal *lex mercatoria digitalis.*

CHAPTER 11

POWER AND POWERLESSNESS IN PUBLIC INSTITUTIONS: THE EXAMPLE OF FINANCIAL STABILITY

CLAUDIA M. BUCH

In many respects 2016 began with a great deal of anxiety: the refugee crisis, the debate about Great Britain's future in the European Union, radical political trends in some European countries, turbulence on the financial markets in emerging nations especially in China—all this has an impact not just on short-term growth. More importantly it poses the question of whether, after a long phase of globalization during which trade and capital flows were liberalized, we might be entering a new phase of protectionism.

About fifteen years ago the former governor of the Reserve Bank of India and Professor at the University of Chicago, Raghuram Rajan, and his co-author Luigi Zingales, described a situation that at first sight might support this conclusion.[1] After a phase of globalization from the end of the 19th to the beginning of the 20th century, there followed a longer phase of nationalization and market partitioning during the interwar period, which was slowly succeeded in the postwar era by a renewed opening up of the markets.

There are many explanations why this reversal of integration and stronger market segmentation took place around one hundred years ago. One important trigger was the serious financial crises of the 1920s. Ailing banks and bank closures, volatile international capital streams, inflationary price trends, and high unemployment—these instabilities and risks undermined people's confidence in the benefits of open markets.

Financial crises have major consequences for both society and the real economy, as opposition to reforms and open markets increases. This can allow "insiders" (according to Rajan and Zingales) to assert themselves more against "outsiders" during the political process, in order to protect their market position. The result, over one hundred years ago, was that the wheel of integration and development of the finance markets was rolled back in the so-called "Great Reversal."

Can we compare this current situation with what was happening at that time? Is there a danger of a similar reversal in world economic integration today, as took place after the financial and economic crises of the 1920s and 1930s? Or have we learned from history?

There are numerous possible answers to these questions. Ultimately neither the economists nor the central banks have conclusive answers. But there is a fundamental difference from the situation in the past, which I would like to discuss in this essay.

After the serious financial crisis that began in 2007, leading to an international banking crisis in 2008/09 and the European debt crisis, the political reaction was not one of national containment, rather it was global (at the level of the G20) and European (in the EU, that is in the Eurozone). For example, significant advances were made: today we have new institutions and new supervisory instruments to make crises less likely in future and to combat them more effectively. We have made progress in reconfiguring the national and international institutional setting. One example is that, in the context of the banking union, at the end of 2014 the European Central Bank assumed supervision of European banks—initially of large, systemically important banks, but it can also take on the supervision of smaller banks.

The banking union is a significant indicator of the creative drive and creative possibilities of policy. Through the union, fundamental competences with regard to the monitoring of banks were transferred from national to European level. In addition, numerous new national and international bodies have the task of analyzing the stability of the global financial system. If required, new macroprudential instruments can be set up to stabilize the financial system.

1. FINANCIAL STABILITY AS A NEW POLICY AREA

After the crisis a new policy area was established—macroprudential monitoring and regulation. It is intended to make the financial system more stable and ensure that financial crises do not unduly affect the real economy. Financial crises have serious economic and social costs: growth falls off, unemployment and sovereign debt rise, and many of these negative effects are long-term. "Financial stability" is thus an important policy objective.

Financial crises are often triggered by excesses in the real-estate markets. Overheating in the real-estate sector, fanned by foreign capital, was an important factor behind the Asian crisis of the late 1990s. Credit-driven price bubbles in real-estate markets in the US and some European countries were a key trigger of the financial crisis of the past. And in Germany, too, real-estate crises such as in Eastern Germany in the 1990s left deep scars on the balance sheets of affected banks and investors. Empirical studies show that recessions in the wake of financial crises caused by the bursting of real-estate price bubbles are more severe and cause a more significant rise in unemployment than "normal" recessions.[2]

There are various channels through which imbalances in the financial sector are transferred to the real economy. What these channels share is that in the first place skewed investment decisions are made: banks and other investors finance areas of the economy that ultimately do not provide sustainable returns. Private households increase their consumption to a level which they cannot finance long term on their current income.

If a price bubble bursts, major write-downs have to be undertaken—banks lose equity capital, households restrict their consumption, and companies reduce their investments. As a result, a negative spiral may occur in which these effects intensify. The financial system no longer fulfills its central tasks: funding no longer flows into the best projects. Risks are not reduced, but are intensified. Central functions such as payment transactions can break down.

Critical developments can become problematic particularly when individual institutions become so large that their imbalances have an impact on the whole system. By implication, therefore, such institutions are protected from bankruptcy, or are "too big to fail." But it is also problematic if institutions are too closely interlinked—"too connected to fail"—or if many market players are exposed to similar risks. For example, many institutions may simultaneously be at risk of an abrupt change in interest rates. Or, many market players—households as well as banks—may be at risk of falling real-estate prices and thus of their securities depreciating. In short, a situation may occur where "too many" institutions are threatened by an imbalance ("too many to fail"). In the expectation of being rescued in an emergency, temptations to take overly high risks may arise once again.

Thus traditional banking supervision acquires the central role of monitoring and regulating risks in the financial system. Regardless of whether systemic risks arise for reasons of size, connectedness, or simultaneous risk exposure, the resulting systemic risks are ultimately all the more significant the greater the microeconomic risks. And banking supervision makes the banks' equity capital requirements a key benchmark, as more equity in the financial system is a crucial factor that gives more stability not only to individual institutions, but also to the entire financial system.

But the crisis has shown that traditional banking supervision offers only part of the answer. The inspection of *individual* institutions provides no answer to the question of the appropriate level of equity capital buffers required to make the financial *system* more stable.

Macroprudential policy therefore has a different kind of objective from microprudential supervision. The task of traditional banking supervision is to monitor banks' compliance with legal regulations. These regulations focus on each individual bank's stability. Macroprudential policy sets its sights on the stability of the entire financial system—it ensures that no systemic risks arise from microeconomic risks, that no incentives for excessive debt arise, and that instabilities in the financial system do not affect real economic growth. It is not about eliminating any fluctuations in the system, but about making sure that the financial system is sufficiently robust that these fluctuations do not adversely impact the real economy.

2. FROM OBJECTIVE VIA INTERIM OBJECTIVE TO INSTRUMENT: THE "POLICY CYCLE"

Few can argue with the abstract objective of "financial stability." The key question is how this objective can be implemented in practice. How can the policy objective of "financial stability" be made tangible? What are the indicators? And how can individual supervisory instruments be implemented?

In practice, the abstract objective of "more financial stability" is broken down into measurable interim objectives and indicators.

The triad of "objective—interim objective—instrument" can be explained by analogy with monetary policy. The mandate of monetary policy is to ensure price stability. Like financial stability, price stability too is not directly measurable. After long academic debates, empirical observations, and experimentation with various monetary policy strategies, many central banks today are focused on inflation. The Governing Council of the European Central Bank, for example, defines price stability as a rate of growth in the Harmonized Index of Consumer Prices of below but near 2%. This represents a measurable interim target. Monetary policy instruments are then used in such a way as to achieve this objective.

What applies to monetary policy also applies to macroprudential regulation. In order to increase the stability of the financial system, providing the banks with adequate equity capital is a concrete interim objective. More equity capital acts as a buffer in the financial system, which helps to cushion risks and to cope with more serious depreciations.

Accordingly, after the crisis the banks' requirements of equity capital were increased. These new equity capital instruments are already available in Germany. Now, increases in equity capital can be demanded if an institution is classified as systemically important in one country or globally. If the lending in one country increases too much, an "anticyclical" capital buffer can be activated. These new macroprudential instruments did not exist before the crisis. Their effectiveness in the individual institution is similar to the effectiveness of microprudential instruments, but their implementation is determined by other policy objectives.

In addition to equity capital requirements, further opportunities for intervention are also possible and in many cases necessary. Financial crises arise from too much debt. Direct restrictions on banks' lending or specific requirements regarding the minimum standards of new lending can therefore stabilize the financial system.

Let us pursue the example of the real-estate market. In Germany, some supervisory instruments are available, which can generally be used to counter risks arising from real-estate transactions. However, their scope of application is very limited, not all financial institutions are covered, and above all, these instruments cannot be used to counteract a possible worsening of lending standards. Primarily they affect the supply of credit, not credit demand. For example, they cannot be used to ensure that a particular borrower contributes a sufficient amount of equity capital to the financing.

Thus supervision in Germany could only counter possible systemically damaging developments in the real-estate market to a limited extent. For this reason, last summer Germany's Financial Stability Committee recommended that legislators create a new legal basis for macroprudential instruments in the real-estate market.[3] Reviewing and, where appropriate, fulfilling of the range of macroprudential instruments is recommended to the national macroprudential authorities by the International Monetary Fund, the Financial Stability Committee, and the European Systemic Risk Board. The recommended instruments are common practice internationally: in addition to numerous emerging countries, currently seventeen EU Member States can set caps on the relationship between the value of a property and the loan taken out on it and the minimum repayments required to service this debt.[4]

These instruments would make it possible to define minimum standards for the granting of loans: for example, as a result of supervision real-estate, finance without any equity capital could be stopped, or a minimum repayment over the credit period could be specified. This would prevent budgets from becoming financially overstretched if a loan is extended and a sudden sharp rise in interest rates then occurs.

For banks that already operate appropriately robust lending, such rules would not be binding and would thus not constitute any restriction. At the same time, however, the banks would be prevented from giving in to excessive competitive pressure and relaxing their lending standards beyond certain limits, thus running excessive risks. It could also prevent price movements on the real-estate market from being regarded too positively or the risks of a turnaround in interest rates being underestimated. Psychological factors and collective misjudgments especially can at times characterize the financial markets, as illustrated by the financial crisis of 2007/08.[5]

The objective of macroprudential policy is therefore to limit the potential impact of collective risk misjudgments on the system as a whole. But like all economic policy interventions, macroprudential measures have side effects that may be unintentional. Or, in the policy process of designing specific instruments, quite different objectives may be introduced which have little to do with the objective of "financial stability." It is therefore necessary to assess regularly the objectives of a regulation and whether these objectives are achieved.

As with monetary policy, financial stability policy should therefore follow a "policy cycle":

1. Availability of data: Adequate data must be available before planning a supervisory measure. This is the only way of assessing how risks develop and whether the implementation of a particular instrument is necessary. This is established practice in monetary policy—numerous statistics regularly produced by the Bundesbank serve as an informational basis for monetary policy decisions.

2. Quantifying the policy objective: As we have already seen, this is the link between the abstract objective of "financial stability" and a measure of the resilience of a system, e.g. its capitalization.

3. Identification of interim objectives: Not all indicators of the stability of a financial system are quickly and easily measurable. Therefore, to implement a stability policy, interim objectives, e.g. credit growth as a whole or in a specific central area such as the real-estate sector, must be defined.

4. Linking instruments and objectives: Before an instrument is activated, an assessment must be made as to what its probable impact will be. Such an *ex-ante* evaluation can be carried out on the basis of various empirical or theoretical models.

5. *Ex-post* evaluation: Once an instrument has been activated, the following can be empirically verified: its impact on the policy objective, what possible side effects and avoidance reactions it has created, and whether it should be adjusted further.

It is this very policy cycle that is laid down in the Financial Stability Committee's recommendation. A key element of this recommendation is the creation of a legal basis for appropriate data. Thus far, official statistics in Germany do not provide any information that is adequate to assess the stability risks in the real-estate sector and to assess the impact of instruments. Currently, our statistics provide information on changes in the volume of credit. These figures show that real-estate loans to private households have risen over the past few years (3.5% in 2015 and 2.4% in 2014). However, in a longer-term comparison, current growth can still be described as moderate. How these loans are secured and the economic sustainability of the households that take out these loans is not systematically recorded, so we know neither the average income nor the average interest rate, neither the credit period, nor the repayment rate. This allows us to say only a very limited amount about the possible stability risks. In view of the fact that real-estate loans to private households account for a good 13% of German banks' balance sheets—with smaller banks such as cooperative banks or savings banks, the proportion is even higher at 30%—this is a knowledge gap that we must close. So far, we have been making do with special surveys that are comparatively expensive and of only limited informational value. It is therefore necessary to systematically record the information that banks already hold about their real-estate loans.

Equally, the Financial Stability Committee's recommendation includes the regular evaluation of the measures. This aspect is particularly relevant because the instruments recommended here are to date unavailable in Germany. There are also very few practical experiences available internationally so far, and knowledge about the effects and side effects is beset with great uncertainty. This necessitates a regular review of the instruments in light of the policy's objectives.

3. THE POWERLESSNESS OF POLICY?

New institutions and new supervisory rules demonstrate that policy can be powerful and can shape in a powerful way. But there are limits to economic action, limits arising from the nature of the markets themselves, and limits resulting from the political process. I would like to look briefly at three of these limits:

1. Fluctuations in the markets cannot be controlled by policy. Even an "optimal" policy cannot and should not have the objective of completely eliminating macroeconomic fluctuations. Dynamism in economic systems—and the growth that results—only emerges when economic actors are able to take risks. However, even when risks become acute, those who can bear them, should do so. Innovation processes and the improvement of productivity and prosperity are associated with fluctuations in the system. The aim of the policy should be to set the framework conditions in

such a way that these fluctuations do not create crises, but lead instead to productive processes. Empirical studies show that this can be successful. Good and stable institutions in particular contribute to a positive relationship between growth and volatility.

2. Policy operates in conditions of uncertainty. Many macroprudential instruments are new and little is known about how they work. What kind of data do we need in order to identify developing instabilities at an early stage? What empirical methods should we use? And, not least, on the basis of which theoretical models can we better understand the effect of supervisory measures? Whether a particular instrument should be activated depends on the answer to these questions. Better analysis can help reduce the resulting uncertainty, but ultimately every decision will have to be made with a considerable degree of uncertainty.

3. Financial stability is subject to political and economic interests. As with any economic decision, there are winners and losers in decisions about the implementation of the new instruments and in improved monitoring of the system. The (supposed) losers are often known, the winners are not. All market players benefit from improved monitoring of the system's stability,

but not all are proportionally involved in the costs of monitoring. If macroprudential instruments are used individual groups will in turn be affected, e.g. young households, who may only be able to afford real-estate financing later on with more equity capital. Winners are the taxpayers, for example, and those who do not lose their jobs because of a recession that is not so deep and protracted after a severe financial crisis.

4. OPPORTUNITIES FOR ACTION IN POLICY

These examples show the limits of macroprudential policy. They do not make the policy "powerless." Rather, the "power" and "powerlessness" of the policy should achieve a sensible balance. I can identify three main approaches here:

1. Structured and transparent policy processes that build on a policy assessment: Macroprudential measures, including the prohibition of certain activities such as short selling, or direct restrictions on banks' pricing, are major market interventions. They are justified only if there is good reason to believe that other instruments are not sufficient to improve the stability of the markets. Therefore, we need a

structured evaluation of policy. What are the objectives of a particular measure? How can these objectives be best achieved? How can we test this? Unlike in previous decades, today we have a much improved infrastructure for evaluating policy measures well. In order to test whether a particular (macroprudential) measure fulfills its objective, microeconomic information is required. Appropriate empirical methods must be available, through which the cause and effect of a measure can be better assessed. Today, in many areas, we have considerably better data infrastructure than before, which is available for analysis. However, we can make even better use of this infrastructure. To this end, we need not only the appropriate legal basis, which makes an evaluation of measures obligatory. We also need, as in the real-estate sector for example, legal bases for collecting additional necessary data. Not least, through a recently accredited research data and service center, the Bundesbank contributes to the availability of an improved infrastructure for the existing data.[6]

2. Better communications: System stability is an abstract concept. The Introduction to the Bundesbank's 2015 *Financial Stability Review* states: "The Bundesbank defines financial stability as a state

in which the key macroeconomic functions, i.e. the allocation of financial resources and risks as well as the settlement of payment transactions, are performed efficiently—particularly in the face of unforeseen events, in stress situations and during periods of structural adjustment." This definition is correct, but it is also very abstract. And whether a policy of financial stability is successful is difficult to measure, because if no serious crises arise, this might be due to the success of the policy, but it might also be just good luck. We are therefore developing measures and indicators on risk-bearing capacity and misplaced incentives in the financial system. And we need an improved social dialogue about how important the objective of "financial stability" is.

3. International coordination: Not least, improved international coordination can help to structure policies better—and perhaps avoid the mistakes of the past. In essence, macroprudential policy is indeed a national task, as the costs of financial crises occur predominantly at national level. But today this national policy is an integral part of an international framework. Comparing the experiences of other countries can help us learn more about the effectiveness of such measures. An extensive exchange of information and experience

takes place through international bodies. Standards are established, which must be maintained by the individual monitors. And the international bodies play an important role in the coordination and evaluation of macroprudential measures. If, for example, a Member State of the European Union wishes to raise equity capital requirements for its banks, the country concerned must notify this measure at European level. This notice contains detailed information on the background, objectives, and possible side effects of the measure. And a comparison with the practices of other countries can help to improve their own institutional framework (peer reviews).

Economic activity takes place in a social context. We have experienced years of liberalization and phases during which the opening up of markets was once again rolled back. Despite the many political challenges we now face, I remain optimistic that we are better equipped today than one hundred years ago. Both the crisis management since the onset of the financial crisis in 2007/08 and the international reform initiatives and institutional changes bear a different hallmark from the developments which, in the past, led to the rolling back of the wheel of globalization and financial market integration.

Notes

1. Cf. Raghuram Rajan and Luigi Zingales, "The Great Reversals: the Politics of Financial Development in the Twentieth Century" in *Journal of Financial Economics, vol. 69 (1) (2003), pp. 5–50.*

2. *Cf. International Monetary Fun* (IMF) Worl* Economic Outlook 2012,* chapter 3, "Dealing with Household Debt", Washington, D.C.

3. https://www.bundesbank.de/Redaktion/DE/ Pressemitteilungen/BBK/2015/2015_06_30_afs.html?nn =1138 (accessed January 2016).

4. Cf. European Systemic Risk Board (ESRB), "A Review of Macro-prudential Policy in the EU One Year after the Introduction of the CRD/CRR," Frankfurt a.M., June 2015.

5. Cf. George A. Akerlof and Robert J. Shiller, *Animal Spirits: How Human Psychology Drives the Economy, an* Why It Matters for Global Capitalism* (Princeton: Princeton University Press, 2009) and Robert J. Shiller, *Irrational Exuberance* (Princeton: Princeton University Press, 2000).

6. Cf. http://www.bundesbank.de/fdsz (accessed January 2016).

CHAPTER 12

AUTHORITY IN THE ART WORLD

HANS ULRICH OBRIST AND RICHARD
WENTWORTH

Excerpt from a conversation between Hans Ulrich Obrist an⸱ Richar⸱ Wentworth

Hans Ulrich Obrist: It's all very exciting. It's September 2016, and we are talking about authority, about power, and how that shifts in the digital age— the transformation of authority. That obviously leads us also to the topic of art education.

Richard Wentworth: Well, I'm more and more aware that artists probably shouldn't come from art schools. They probably shouldn't even come—it's a funny thing to be saying, but I wonder if artists shouldn't be coming —artists will come from where they come from, but actually when you look at most— if you look at a sweep of—artists and you examine their biographies, there's often very interesting complexity in that they're not tidy, they didn't come out of some career structure.

Maybe even the word artist has a small "a", so how somebody's desire meets what we might call "means of production" is still very puzzling—how we say we recognize when people are good at something, or we even say people are drawn to something. We certainly recognize people who are no good at anything, not at anything; no good at something. There's something odd about this. I wonder if what I'm actually trying to articulate is that I wonder what happened to the idea that artists come out of guilds.

In the Middle Ages we had systems of professionalization, where you would become a subscriber to a particular guild and that guild was distinct. The leatherworkers were not the brush makers, and the brush makers were not the silver workers. In the Renaissance you had people who would jump across everything, like Cellini or Michelangelo. But there's something very odd now. Somebody said to me last week—somebody who had been a student in Switzerland, and you would understand this—they said that they'd been a student in the applied arts.

HUO: Yes, because there's no art school there.

RW: Well, then they said it was very difficult to move from the applied arts to the fine arts. So I said "Why?" She said there's a sort of social impediment or some kind of...

HUO: An obstacle?

RW: Something like that, and obviously intellectually this person doesn't see themselves as confined in that way. Already these are questions of power. They're questions of authority or readings of authority, the speed with which somebody will notice perhaps where somebody studied. What I would call the hidden letters after people's names, but actually artists aren't interesting because they've got letters after their names.

If you're on a train journey with an artist, or with anybody, you find out their field of energy. Clearly I am saying something which is anti-professional. I'm then immediately nervous of the problem of the grand amateur, because I'm an Englishman[1]. But there's something very strange happening to do with this professionalization and that comes, of course, with internationalization and globalization.

Perceptions of authority, perceptions of canons of where people studied. But of course what we find out, often later and often after people are dead, is who was friends of whom and how those friendships worked—in fact the pleasure of knowing Bill Berkson[2] was that he could talk about Frank O'Hara[3] and Guston[4] with an easy experiential intimacy that to my knowledge wasn't... I don't know how they had met or they would know each other but...

HUO: But it's fascinating because in a way we think of cause, I mean the digital age, if you look, for example, at blockchain and the whole idea of a blockchain...

RW: What if I tell you I don't know what that is?

HUO: It's this new currency idea, that we no longer need banks. Through a digital protocol it's basically possible that something happens between two individuals, that a transaction happens between two individuals. You're really cutting out the middle-man or the middle-woman in a way, which is something that happens, I think, strongly in the digital age. I think in a way it's kind of interesting because it also leads back to this question of whether the artist is dependent on schools or galleries or auction houses, because in a way it's kind of interesting because this has existed. This DIY approach has existed in the arts for a long time, as we know, before the Internet.

I did "The Kitchen Show" and came to see you in the late 1980s, early 1990s. There was no Internet. The actual drawing you made at the time on a paper napkin suggested how an exhibition can be completely self-organized without much, and then become a room or travel. It was already there. Looking at this drawing the other day, I kind of thought: he was in the age of the Internet when you drew that kitchen drawing... I basically agree with Tom Sachs who said you've kind of invented Instagram before Instagram, which is why also *Making Do an Getting By*[5] was such an urgent book to do. To cut a long story short, it would just be great to hear you talk a little bit about this field.

RW: I think a good way of doing that is to talk about lack. [...] There are the things we lack, things which we might perceive in other people. We often desire other people because they appear to have something that we want. But there's also learning to make luck.

I am exceptionally gregarious. I don't want to be at parties all the time, I don't like what I call constructed gregariousness particularly, but I like my fellow humans and I like the moment of encounter. I think what that used to mean was that I would send people postcards, which probably meant I wish I knew them better. So they weren't love letters, but they were—I will have sent you postcards, I don't know. Then there's a period where the postcard starts to die.

HUO: Sometimes you would glue things on postcards.

RW: I don't know whether I did so much of that, but I don't think...

HUO: I have a sentence your son wrote glued on a postcard.

RW: Okay, that's possible, but my children adored you, so you were a fable in their childhood. So there you have it, there you have it. You're not part of their... You didn't attend their school, but you were a feature in their life as were lots of other people around and near art.

But I think that gregariousness is attached, in my case, to anxiety. It's quite risky to speak to people if you don't quite know what you're going to say. There's this suggestion that I have mild Tourette's. Perhaps I do, but I don't think I've ever done anyone any harm. The energy, the space between people can only really be cultural. That transaction is—and the transaction is more like—the moment you move out of your own language. It's much more complicated. Our conversation this morning is full of little mis-hearings and misapprehensions, most of which we trust each other enough to make into energy.

What I'm trying to describe is I think that's a reflective and a reflexive space. So I think if you meet people who might be equal and opposite, or people who give back, then you end up with a condition that might be called correspondence, people who are responsive. I'm sure that for every person who responds to me there is somebody walking in the opposite direction.

HUO: I'm interested in the study of lack, because I spoke the other day to Joseph Grigely[6] in Chicago, and I was wondering... With Joseph being deaf since the age of eleven, and email having been for him a great relief, he was one of the early adopters of email because it allowed him to communicate in such an easy way. Yet he has never created an artwork with email because he says it's too complete. You have an email exchange with someone, it's all there, it's a complete email exchange.

The beauty of these little handwritten notes, which he composed his conversation of, is that there is something missing that creates a desire. So in a way, I think it's interesting to think about how that changes in the digital age.

Notes

1. On dilettantism, Englishness and the tradition of English philosophical empiricism, see, for example, Elisa Tamarkin, *Anglophilia* (Chicago: Chicago University Press, 2007), pp. 273–4.

2. Bill Berkson (1939–2016) was a US poet, critic, teacher, and sometime curator. He was professor emeritus at the San Francisco Art Institute, where, between 1984 and 2008, he taught art history, art writing, and poetry.

3. Frank O'Hara (1926–1966) was a US writer, poet, art critic, and a curator at the Museum of Modern Art, New York.

4. Philip Guston (1913–1980) was a Canadian painter and printmaker.

5. Richard Wentworth, *Making Do and Getting By* (Cologne: Verlag Walther Koenig, 2015).

6. Joseph Grigely is a US artist (1956–) who creates art from the written conversations that he has in his daily life.

CONTRIBUTORS

Prof. Dr. Claudia M. Buch is Deputy President of the Deutsche Bundesbank. She is responsible for the Financial Stability Department, the Statistics Department, and the Audit Department. Professor Buch is the accompanying person of the President of the Bundesbank on the ECB Governing Council and a member of the German Financial Stability Committee (FSC). From 1985 to 1991 she studied economics at the University of Bonn, graduating from the University of Wisconsin with a Master of Business Administration degree in 1988. She worked at the Institute for World Economics in Kiel (IfW) (1992–2013). During that time she gained her post-doctoral qualification at the University of Kiel (2002) after receiving her doctorate there in 1996. She was

Professor of Economics for International Finance and Macroeconomics at the University of Tübingen (2004–13) and Scientific Director at the Institute for Applied Economic Research (IAW) there (2005–13). Prior to joining the Bundesbank in May 2014, she was the President of the Institute for Economic Research (IWH) in Halle (2013–14) and Professor of Economics at the Otto von Guericke University Magdeburg (2013–14). From 2012 to 2014 she was a member of the German Council of Economic Experts.

Dr. Corinne Michaela Flick studied both law and literature, taking American studies as her subsidiary. She gained her Dr. Phil. in 1989. She has worked as in-house lawyer for Bertelsmann Buch AG and Amazon.com. In 1998 she became General Partner in Vivil GmbH und Co. KG, Offenburg. She is Founder and Chair of the Convoco Foundation. Dr. Flick is Co-Founder of the Friends of the Bavarian State Library, Munich, a member of the Executive Committee of the International Council of the Tate Gallery, London, and was Chair of the Board of Trustees of the Aspen Institute Germany from 2012 to 2016.

Prof. Dr. Dr. h.c. Clemens Fuest gained his doctorate at the University of Cologne in 1994 and his postdoctoral qualification at Ludwig-Maximilian University, Munich, in 2000. From 2001 he was Professor of Political Economy at the University of Cologne, from 2004 Visiting Professor at Bocconi University in Milan, and 2008–13 Professor of Business Taxation and Research Director of the Oxford University Centre for Business Taxation. Between 2013 and 2015, he was President and Director of Science and Research of the Centre for European Economic Research (ZEW) and Professor of Economics at the University of Mannheim.

Since 2016 he has been President of the Ifo Institute for Economic Research in Munich.

Clemens Fuest has been a member of the Academic Advisory Board of the German Federal Ministry of Finance since 2003 and Head of the Board 2007–10. In October 2012 he became a member of the Advisory Board for Sustainable Development of the State Government of Baden-Württemberg. He has been a member of The Market Economy Foundation's scientific council *Kronberger Kreis* 2004–08, and again as of March 2013. Since 2014 he has been a member of the EU High-Level Group on Own Resources, and since 2015 a member of the German Minimum Wage

Commission. He is Programme Director of the Oxford University Centre for Business Taxation, a member of numerous German and international scientific academies and associations, and is on the board of the International Institute for Public Finance. He is editor of *Beiträge zur Finanzwissenschaft* [Contributions to Financial Research] and on several editorial boards of scientific journals.

Prof. Dr. Thomas Hoeren studied theology and law at the Universities of Tübingen, Münster, and London 1980–87. In 1989 he gained his doctorate, and in 1994 his postdoctoral qualification from Münster University. In 1995–97 he was Professor at the Faculty of Law of the Heinrich Heine University, Düsseldorf. In 1996–2012 he was a part-time judge at the Düsseldorf Appeal Court. Since April 1997 he has been Professor of Information, Media and Business Law at the University of Münster and Head of the Institute for Information, Telecommunication and Media Law (ITM). He is Adjunct Professor at the Fraunhofer Institute for Applied Information Technology (FIT). He is a domain-name arbitrator for the World Intellectual Property Organization (WIPO) and the European Commission. In 2012–14 he was Dean of the Faculty of Law at Münster University. His professional appointments and memberships include: Research Fellow at the Oxford Internet Institute, Balliol College in 2004; Lecturer in Information and IT Law at the Universities of Zurich and Vienna; Member of the Expert Committee for Copyright and Publishing Law at the German Union for Intellectual Property Protection; since 2006 personal tutor at the Studienstiftung des Deutschen Volkes; in 2005 he received the Alcatel-SEL Foundation research prize for "technical communication". Since April 2015 he has been a spokesman for the Federal Ministry of Education and Research's major research project ABIDA (Assessing Big Data).

Prof. Dr. Peter M. Huber gained his Ph.D. Dr. jur. in 1987 and his postdoctoral qualification in constitutional and administrative law in 1991. He was Professor of Public Law in Augsburg. In 1992–2001 he was Professor of Constitutional and Administrative Law, European Law, Public, Commercial, and Environmental Law in Jena. He was Chair of Public Law and European Integration Law in Bayreuth from 2001 to 2002. Since 2002 he has held the Chair of Public Law and Political Philosophy in Munich.

From 2009 to 2010 Professor Huber was Interior Minister for Thuringia, and in 2010 he was made a Judge in Germany's Federal Constitutional Court.

Among his publications are: *Grunⁱrechtsschutz ⁱurch Organisation unⁱ Verfahren als Kompetenzproblem in ⁱer Gewaltenteilung unⁱ im Bunⁱesstaat* (1987); *Konkurrenzschutz im Verwaltungsrecht* (1991); *Recht ⁱer Europäischen Integration* (second edition, 2002); *Klarere Verantwortungsteilung von Bunⁱ, Länⁱern unⁱ Kommunen?* (2004); *Staat unⁱ Wissenschaft* (2008); *Beiträge zu Juristenausbilⁱung unⁱ Hochschulrecht* (2010). He is Joint Editor of the *Hanⁱbuch Ius Publicum Europaeum*, vols. I–IV (2007–11).

Prof. Dr. Kai A. Konrad is Director at the Max Planck Institute for Tax Law and Public Finance and a Scientific Member of the Max Planck Society. Previously he was a Full Professor of Economics at the Freie Universität Berlin from 1994 to 2009. Concurrently he was a Director at the Wissenschaftszentrum Berlin für Sozialforschung (WZB) from 2001 to 2009. He is member of the German National Academy of Sciences Leopoldina and of four other science academies. He is a Co-editor of the Journal of Public Economics. Since 1999 he has been a member of the Council of Scientific

Advisors to the Federal Ministry of Finance and was the Chair from 2011 to 2014.

Prof. Dr. Stefan Korioth gained his doctorate in law in 1990 and completed his postdoctoral qualification in public and constitutional law. From 1996 to 2000 he was Professor of Public Law, Constitutional History, and Theory of Government at Greifswald. In 2000 he accepted the Chair of Public and Ecclesiastical Law at LMU, Munich. His publications include *Integration uni Buniesstaat* (1990), *Der Finanzausgleich zwischen Buni uni Läniern* (1997), *Gruniizüge ies Staatskirchenrechts* (with B. Jean d'Heur, 2000), and *Das Buniesverfassungsgericht* (with Klaus Schlaich, 9th edition, 2012).

Dr. Peter Maurer was born in Thun, Switzerland, in 1956. He studied history and international law in Bern, where he was awarded a doctorate. In 1987 he entered the Swiss diplomatic service, where he held various positions in Bern and Pretoria before being transferred to New York in 1996 as Deputy Permanent Observer at the Swiss mission to the United Nations. In 2000 he was appointed Ambassador and Head of the Human Security Division in the political directorate of the Swiss Department of Foreign Affairs in Bern.

In 2004 Dr. Maurer was appointed Ambassador and Permanent Representative of Switzerland to the United Nations in New York. In this position, he worked to integrate Switzerland, which had only recently joined the United Nations, into multilateral networks. In June 2009, the UN General Assembly elected Dr. Maurer Chairman of the Fifth Committee, in charge of administrative and budgetary affairs. In addition, he was elected Chairman of the Burundi configuration of the UN Peacebuilding Commission. In January 2010 Dr. Maurer was appointed Secretary of State for Foreign Affairs in Bern and took over the reins of the Swiss Department of Foreign Affairs, with its five directorates and some 150 Swiss diplomatic missions around the world. He succeeded Jakob Kellenberger as ICRC President on July 1, 2012.

Hans Ulrich Obrist is Co-Director of the Serpentine Galleries, London. Prior to this, he was curator of the Musée d'Art Moderne de la Ville, Paris. Since his first show *Worl* Soup (The Kitchen Show)* in 1991 he has curated more than 250 exhibitions. In 2009 Obrist was made Honorary Fellow of the Royal Institute of British Architects (RIBA), and in 2011 received the CCS Bard Award for Curatorial Excellence. Obrist has lectured internationally

at academic and art institutions, and is contrib-
uting editor to several magazines and journals.
Obrist's recent publications include *A Brief History of
Curating, Everything You Always Wante to Know About
Curating But Were Afrai to Ask, Do It: The Compen ium,
Think Like Clou s, Ai Weiwei Speaks, Ways of Curating,*
and new volumes of his *Conversation Series.*

Dr. Stefan Oschmann has been Chairman of the
Executive Board and CEO of Merck since May 2016.
Previously, Stefan Oschmann served as the Vice-
Chairman and Deputy CEO. In this role he was responsible for strategy development of the Merck Group. He
joined Merck in 2011 as CEO of the Biopharma division and member of the Executive Board. From 2013
to 2014 he was responsible for the healthcare business
sector of Merck. In that role he oversaw the Biopharma,
Consumer Health, Allergopharma, and Biosimilars
businesses. Before joining Merck, he worked for the US
pharma company MSD, where he served as President of
Emerging Markets. Other positions included member
of senior management and corporate officer with
responsibility for the business in Europe, the Middle
East, Africa, and Canada; Senior Vice-President in
charge of Worldwide Human Health Marketing as well
as Vice-President of Europe and the German business.

He started his career at the International Atomic Energy Agency (IAEA) in 1985, before moving to the German Animal Health Federation (BfT), a member association of the German Chemical Industry Association (VCI), in 1987. He studied veterinary medicine at Ludwig-Maximilian University, Munich from 1977 to 1982 and earned a doctorate there in 1985.

Prof. Dr. Christoph G. Paulus studied law at Munich, taking his doctorate in law in 1980. His post-doctoral qualification, gained in 1991, was in civil law, civil procedure, and Roman law, for which he was awarded the Medal of the University of Paris II. He received his LL.M. at Berkeley in 1983/1984 and returned to Berkeley between 1989 and 1990 as a recipient of a Feodor Lynen Stipend from the Humboldt Foundation. In 1992–94 he was Associate Professor at Augsburg, and from the summer semester 1994 he was at the Law Faculty of the Humboldt University in Berlin, becoming Dean of the Faculty in 2008–10. In 2009 he was made Director of the Research Center Institute for Interdisciplinary Restructuring, and Consultant to the International Monetary Fund and the World Bank. Among other roles he is member (and Director) of the International Insolvency Institute of the American College of Bankruptcy and the

International Association for Procedural Law. Since 2006 he has been advisor on insolvency law to the German delegation to UNCITRAL. He is on the editorial board of the *Zeitschrift für Wirtschaftsrecht* (ZIP), the *Norton Annual Review of International Insolvency*, and the *International Insolvency Law Review*, among other journals.

Prof. Dr. Dr. h.c. Wolfgang Schön studied law and economics studies at the University of Bonn, and was awarded his doctorate at Bonn in 1985. In 1992 he received his postdoctoral qualification in civil law, commercial, corporate, and tax law in Bonn. He was Professor at the University of Bielefeld from 1992 to 1996, and Director of the Institute for Tax Law and of the Centre of European Commercial Law, Bonn, from 1996 to 2002. Since 2002 he has been Director and Scientific Member of the Max Planck Institute for Intellectual Property, Competition, and Tax Law in Munich. He has been Honorary Professor of Civil, Commercial, Corporate, and Tax Law at Ludwig-Maximilian University, Munich, since 2002. From 2008 to 2014 Professor Schön was Vice-President of the Max Planck Society. Since 2014 he has been Vice-President of the German Research Foundation (DFG).

Prof. Sir Roger Scruton, Ph.D. is currently a Senior Research Fellow of Blackfriars Hall, Oxford, and Senior Fellow at the Ethics and Public Policy Center, Washington DC. He was for a while employed by Birkbeck College in the University of London, but since 1990 has been self-employed. He is author of over 40 books, including works of criticism, political theory, and aesthetics, as well as novels and short stories. His writings include *The Aesthetics of Music* (1997), *Death-Devoteı Heart: Sex anı the Sacreı in Wagner's Tristan anı Isolıe* (2003), *Unıerstanıing Music* (2009), *The Face of Goı* (2011), *The Soul of the Worlı* (2014), and *Notes from Unıergrounı* (2014). Roger Scruton is a Fellow of the Royal Society of Literature, a Fellow of the European Academy of Arts and Sciences, and a Fellow of the British Academy.

Richard Wentworth has lived and worked in London since 1965. He became Master of Drawing at the Ruskin School of Drawing and Fine Art, Oxford University, and between 2009 and 2011 was Professor and Head of the Royal College of Art's Sculpture Department. His work, encircling the notion of objects and their use as part of our day-to-day experiences, has altered the traditional definition of sculpture as well as photography. By transforming and manipulating industrial and/or found objects into works of art, Wentworth subverts their original function and extends our understanding of them by breaking the conventional system of classification. In photography, as in the ongoing series *Making Do an¢ Getting By*, Wentworth documents the everyday, paying attention to objects, occasional and involuntary geometries, as well as uncanny situations that often go unnoticed. Major solo presentations include *Bol¢ Ten¢encies*, Peckham, London, UK (2015), *Black Maria with Gruppe*, Kings Cross, London, UK (2013), Whitechapel Gallery, London, UK (2010), 52nd Venice Biennale, Venice, Italy (2009), TATE, Liverpool, UK (2005), Artangel, London, UK (2002), Bonner Kunstverein, Bonn, Germany (1998), Stedelijk Museum, Amsterdam, The Netherlands (1994), Serpentine Gallery, London, UK (1993).

POWER AND ITS PARADOXES
2016

ISBN: 978-0-9931953-2-7

With contributions by: Clemens Fuest, Thomas Hoeren, Wolfgang Ischinger, Stefan Korioth, Hans Ulrich Obrist and Simon Denny, Christoph G. Paulus, Albrecht Ritschl, Jörg Rocholl, Roger Scruton, Brennan Simms

TO DO OR NOT TO DO—INACTION AS A FORM OF ACTION
2015

ISBN: 978-0-9931953-0-3

With contributions by: Bazon Brock, Gert-Rudolf Flick, Peter M. Huber, Kai A. Konrad, Stefan Korioth, Friedhelm Mennekes, Hans Ulrich Obrist and Marina Abramović, Christoph G. Paulus, Jörg Rocholl, Wolfgang Schön, Roger Scruton, Pirmin Stekeler-Weithofer

DEALING WITH DOWNTURNS: STRATEGIES IN UNCERTAIN TIMES
2014

ISBN: 978-0-9572958-8-9

With contributions by: Jens Beckert, Bazon Brock, Saul Davi, Ger* Gigerenzer, Paul Kirchhof, Kai A. Konra*, Stefan Korioth, Christoph G. Paulus, Jörg Rocholl, Burkhar* Schwenker*

COLLECTIVE LAW-BREAKING—A THREAT TO LIBERTY
2013

ISBN: 978-0-9572958-5-8

With contributions by: Shaukat Aziz, Rolan Berger, Christoph G. Paulus, Ingolf Pernice, Wolfgang Schön, Hannes Siegrist, Jürgen Stark, Pirmin Stekeler-Weithofer*

WHO OWNS THE WORLD'S KNOWLEDGE?
2012

ISBN: 978-0-9572958-0-3

With contributions by: Eckhard Cordes, Urs Gasser, Thomas Hoeren, Viktor Mayer-Schönberger, Christoph G. Paulus, Jürgen Renn, Burkhard Schwenker and Hannes Siegrist

CAN'T PAY, WON'T PAY? SOVEREIGN DEBT AND THE CHALLENGE OF GROWTH IN EUROPE
2011

ISBN: 978-0-9572958-3-4

With contributions by: Roland Berger, Howard Davies, Otmar Issing, Paul Kirchhof, Kai A. Konrad, Stefan Korioth, Christoph G. Paulus and Burkhard Schwenker